TRADITIONS

of the

ANCIENTS

MARCIA FORD

TRADITIONS
of the
ANCIENTS

Vintage Faith Practices
for the 21st Century

BROADMAN
& HOLMAN
PUBLISHERS
NASHVILLE, TENNESSEE

Ten-Digit ISBN: 0–8054–4076-3
Thirteen-Digit ISBN: 978–0–8054–4076-8

Published by Broadman & Holman Publishers
Nashville, Tennessee

Dewey Decimal Classification: 270.1
Subject Heading: CHURCH HISTORY–30-600, EARLY
CHURCH
RITES AND CEREMONIES / CHRISTIAN LIFE
Scripture versions are identified by acronym as follows: CEV, the
Contemporary English Version, © American Bible Society 1991,
1992; used by permission. HCSB, *Holman Christian Standard Bible*®
Copyright © 1999, 2000, 2002, 2004 by Holman Bible Publishers.
Used by permission. KJV, King James Version. MSG, *The Message,*
the New Testament in Contemporary English, © 1993 by Eugene H.
Peterson, published by NavPress, Colorado Springs, Colo. NASB, New
American Standard Bible, © the Lockman Foundation, 1960, 1962,
1963, 1968, 1971, 1972, 1973, 1975, 1977; used by permission. NIV,
the Holy Bible, New International Version, copyright © 1973, 1978,
1984 by International Bible Society. NKJV, New King James Version,
copyright © 1979, 1980, 1982, Thomas Nelson, Inc., Publishers.
NLT, the *Holy Bible,* New Living Translation, copyright © 1996. Used
by permission of Tyndale House Publishers, Inc., Wheaton, Illinois
60189. All rights reserved. NRSV, New Revised Standard Version of
the Bible, copyright © 1989 by the Division of Christian Education
of the National Council of Churches of Christ in the United States
of America, used by permission, all rights reserved. RSV, Revised
Standard Version of the Bible, copyrighted 1946, 1952, © 1971, 1973.

1 2 3 4 5 6 7 8 9 10 11 12 15 14 13 12 11 10 09 08 07 06

Tradition means giving votes to the most obscure of all classes—our ancestors. It is the democracy of the dead. Tradition refuses to submit to the small and arrogant oligarchy of those who merely happen to be walking around.

—G. K. CHESTERTON

Contents

Beginnings

The first house my husband and I ever owned was a small, two-story Victorian in Ocean Grove, New Jersey, a seaside town that still holds annual Methodist camp meetings and manages to stage a host of religious events despite its decidedly secular location on the Jersey Shore. We loved that hundred-year-old house and that quaint and quirky little town, and making the decision to leave both was one of the toughest things we've had to do as a married couple.

Not long after we had gotten settled in our new home in another state, I began having recurring dreams about the house we left behind. I'll spare you the irrelevant minutiae—few things, I've learned, are more boring than hearing someone describe in excruciating detail dreams that are essentially indescribable. Often, that someone has been me, and I've even bored myself.

The theme of this recurring dream is apparently a universal one, that of discovering new and fascinating rooms. In my dream, I return to the Ocean

Grove house, and the new owner shows me all the changes she's made. It's depressing, because in real life she had a truckload of money, which means in my dream life she was able to make all the improvements the house sorely needed. Worst of all was the attic, which in reality was a tiny storage area. In my dream, however, entering the attic is like entering the Narnia wardrobe: there's a whole other world there that I never knew existed, one filled with wonder and mystery and joy. But neither the attic nor the house belongs to me any longer. I have unknowingly handed all that wonder and mystery and joy over to someone else; all I can do is berate myself for never exploring the hidden corners of that attic when I had the opportunity.

That unexplored attic stands as a symbol for much of my life with God. After coming to faith in Christ in 1972—and anticipating a life filled with wonder and mystery and joy—I settled for what has been a good but restless life with God. I had questions, so many questions, but I learned early on that asking them would get me in huge vats of hot water with church leadership. We evangelicals not only had an agreed-upon statement of faith, which I adhered to and still do adhere to, but also an agreed-upon way of doing church. It was this latter situation that made me restless. Something about our way of expressing our faith was failing to meet my deepest spiritual needs. I would read about the early church and long for what they had, but I reached the conclusion that we couldn't expect to have even a semblance of what they had.

And then I began to explore the hidden recesses of the attic where we evangelicals had stored the treasures of church life down through the centuries. It was in some ways like opening the wardrobe door to Narnia. This whole other world of ritual and tradition was home to both Aslan and the White Witch, and it wasn't always clear at first whether these practices led to the good lion or the evil queen. But the good lion is a faithful leader, and he can be trusted to help us sort the genuine treasures from the religious rubbish.

Part of what I discovered in that attic were documents showing that the early years of the Christian church were a time of tremendous diversity of belief and practice. That diversity continued even after the formative church councils of the fourth and fifth centuries had standardized church life to some extent. During those first centuries, followers of Christ experienced perhaps the greatest freedom of expression with regard to their faith that the church has ever known. To be sure, their freedom resulted in some doctrines and rituals that were later considered to be unorthodox, but it also gave birth to a creative faith within the bounds of orthodoxy that we can draw on today to enhance our own spirituality.

Consider the following:

- A wealthy Egyptian named Antony was the first Christian monk, according to historical accounts. Upon his conversion, he left his wealth behind and fled to the desert to do battle with Satan and his minions. Antony had more than a few peculiar habits, including praying with his arms extended outward mimicking the shape of the cross—for hours, even days, at a time. This practice was imitated by others and became known among desert dwellers as the Vigil of the Cross.

- A fifth-century ascetic named Simon Stylites sought solitude so he could pray without ceasing. But he became something of a roadside attraction and was forced to keep moving and retreating deeper into the desert. Eventually, he began building towers to escape the crowds that came to see him. He lived atop various pillars, the highest at sixty feet, for thirty-six years, spending most of his time pacing and praying.

- A fourth-century woman now known as Egeria did the unthinkable for a woman of her era: she spent three years visiting all the sites associated with biblical history and the life of Christ, climbing mountains, sleeping wherever she could, and leaving a highly detailed, written account of her journeys. The record of her trip is the first known formal writing by a woman.

What can Christians in the third millennium learn from these and other ancient examples of faith? By today's standards, some, such as Antony and Simon, would be considered eccentric, while others lived out their faith in questionable ways. Can they possibly teach us anything of value?

I believe they can. In fact, they already have, because they have taught me a great deal that is of value. As a journalist, I have lived and worked according to a number of sound research principles, including the principle of going straight to the source—in this case, the early church—for a fuller understanding of an issue, an event, or a practice. With regard to my faith, that has meant exploring the world of the earliest Christians, and the church's Judaic roots, in order to enrich my own faith experience. What I learned from the ancients has deepened my own faith experience and given me countless hours of reflection—and amusement.

That is not to imply that the early Christians always got it right. Far from it. The ancient church—which I define as the church through the sixth century and the crumbling of the Roman Empire—certainly had its share of issues and questions to grapple with and was hardly the institution it is today. But in that climate of diverse perspectives, chaos and confusion, individual believers had the freedom to express their faith with a creativity we seldom see today.

We're so sure of what it means to be Christian—how we're supposed to behave and how we're supposed to worship—that we rarely venture out of our spiritual comfort zones. The beauty of the early church, by contrast, lies in the very fact that there was no comfort zone, no carefully crafted formula for living out the Christian life. Certainly, early Christians had access to the teachings about that life in the apostolic writings, and by the end of the fourth century they even had a relatively agreed-upon canon of Scripture, but beyond that, faith was a fairly free enterprise.

No one had come along yet to tell believers that they should "dress nice" for the 11:00 a.m. service on Sunday. In fact, no one bothered to tell the desert dwellers that they should bathe once in a while; it would have done no good, because they considered bathing to be sinfully self-centered. No one had told them yet that they needed to schedule a daily quiet time and spend fifteen minutes each morning at their devotions, nor had they been told that they should create an ongoing prayer list. For many, the whole of their interior life was their "quiet time," and they saw every moment of their lives as their devotional time and as unceasing prayer to God.

In *Traditions of the Ancients,* I reflect on these practices in light of their helpfulness to believers today, a time when contemporary Christians are seeking new ways to connect with God. By "these practices," I specifically mean those that can provide an added dimension to our lives. Many of the ancient practices died for good reason, and I'm hardly one who thinks that because something is old, it has to be good. No, the ancients did some pretty wacky things at times, and while I'm not disinclined to do wacky things myself, some bizarre spiritual exercises are best left unresurrected.

What, then, is the point of reviving these ancient rituals and traditions? In my own life, I've found three reasons for adopting and adapting these historical practices for contemporary use:

1. *They add depth and richness to our life with God.* One of the characteristics of the expression of our faith in Christ today is a yearning for a deeper relationship with God—a relationship that transcends our church life and occupies our every waking moment. The Barna Research Group points to a seismic change in the way we do church and the way we live out our personal relationship with God. This change, ironically, is in part characterized by a "back to the future" mentality. By returning to the very practices we once discarded, many of us have discovered and continue to discover the level of intimacy with God that we've been longing for.

2. *They provide a solid foundation as we explore different ways to express our faith.* While the current model for church services and church life will likely survive these changes to some degree and for some time, for many of us our personal relationship with God will undergo a radical transformation despite our church experience. What I mean is that if the typical service—a couple of songs, welcome and announcements, offering, communion, sermon, closing song—doesn't do it for us anymore, we can draw on practices that were rich in meaning to our spiritual ancestors and adapt them for our use today. The biblical or historical basis for the practice becomes an anchor as we use the concept behind the practice to discover God in new and fresh ways.

3. *They unite us with believers in the past as well as our contemporaries.* In the heady days of the Jesus People Movement, we sensed a nearly tangible connection with the first followers of Christ. We believed we were the first-century church come to twentieth-century America, and we felt more at home with our spiritual counterparts in the New Testament than we did with our modern counterparts who suffered week after week in a lifeless congregation. We were a bit arrogant—we were going to show them how to really live the Christian life—but we believed we had genuinely found that "something more" which seemed to have eluded the church for so long, and we wanted to share it.

Fast forward thirty years. In the intervening time, many of us who identified with progressive evangelicalism settled for a shadow of the life with God that we had envisioned. We're finally recapturing that vision and experiencing that life by learning from the ancients, but there's more. Lo and behold, we're also learning from our contemporaries in liturgical churches that have kept many of these meaningful practices alive for centuries.

Some of those practices have been abused, to be sure. Others have lost their spiritual value as the passing of time has obscured the profound meaning behind their birth. Still others—like, say, meditation—have become so closely associated with religions outside the Judeo-Christian tradition that we have fled from the practices out of a misguided fear that our faith would somehow become tainted.

Today, though, evangelicalism has grown up and recognized those fears as misguided. We're reading the ancients and talking to the liturgicals, and our faith is all the richer for it. We're exploring those once-hidden corners and discovering doorways that open up to that whole other world of wonder and mystery and joy.

There's a lot of overlap in the traditions you'll be reading about: the Jesus Prayer folds into unceasing prayer, which can be integrated into manual labor, a hallmark of many who practiced asceticism in silence and solitude. Asceticism, in fact, encompasses most of these practices. But by breaking them out into individual components, I'm hoping I've given you a varied selection of spiritual exercises that you can choose from and adapt to your own style of worshiping God.

Do I practice all twenty-eight spiritual exercises that follow? No way. Neither does anyone else I know or even know of. But I have practiced or at least attempted to practice all but a few that were not relevant to my life when I discovered them (such as memorial meals). Some resonated with my way of worshiping God, while others did not.

You're likely to have a similar experience. So go ahead—explore the treasures of spiritual practice that we've kept in the attic for too long. You may just discover a whole new dimension to your life with God.

Chapter 1

A Theology of Tears

Many of us recall coming to Christ in a moment of overwhelming grief and joy, watered by a massive profusion of tears. So profound was that moment for me that I was unable to utter a word. Hours later, alone in my room and far from the friends who had escorted me into the kingdom of God, I panicked. Had I done it right? I hadn't prayed the legendary "sinner's prayer"; was I truly saved? I recall the next scene that night with a mixture of sadness and amusement—me, on the floor by my bed, begging Jesus to come into my life. As if he hadn't.

My behavior that night would have bewildered Evagrius Ponticus and his fellow desert dwellers, and not just because of the obvious language barrier. To them, tears were the utmost sign of true repentance. There could be no genuine repentance without tears, they believed, nor could there be any possibility of going deeper into the heart of God until you were "cried out," to use a current phrase.

To the ancients, the state of brokenness that yields tears was something to continually strive for—or better, perhaps, a gift to seek—throughout your life. They saw the tears of conversion as a prelude to a lifetime of weeping tears of purification as you more deeply desired to draw near to God. Your natural separation from God caused by your sinfulness, and your supernatural longing for oneness with God, would in due time prompt a deluge of tears, if that longing were authentic. The tears were not the goal but the expected result, the evidence of your brokenness before God.

Bear in mind that to our spiritual ancestors, getting to the point where you were cried out took *days.* John Climacus, who headed up a monastery at Mount Sinai in the sixth century, compared this state to weeping like a baby, but I'm not so sure that's an appropriate analogy. Babies generally cry to call attention to an immediate need and usually stop when that need is met or they've run out of steam. Weeping tears of purification, as I understand it, is nearly uncontrollable. There's no running out of steam, no superficial need that can be met to dam the floodgate of tears.

Evagrius advocated praying for the gift of tears to "soften the savage hardness in your soul." He and others also saw the tears of purification as a means of allowing the light of God to penetrate the darkness that still lurks inside you. They saw the eyes as the windows to the soul and the tears of repentance and sorrow as a means of clearing the way to a new and deeper understanding of God. In *Soul Making,* author Alan Jones adds that the

---

Tears are nature's lotion for the eyes.
The eyes see better for being washed by them.

—CHRISTIAN NEVELL BOVEE

desert dwellers likened tears to the rite of baptism and therefore resurrection, restoring the "disfigured soul" to its authentic state. Symeon the New Theologian, an Eastern Orthodox monk who lived centuries after Evagrius, described them as "tears that clean the darkness of my mind."

"The fruits of the inner man begin only with the shedding of tears," wrote Isaac of Nineveh in the seventh century. "When you reach the place of tears, then know that your spirit has come out from the prison of this world and has set its foot upon the [earthly] path that leads toward the [other world]. Your spirit begins at this moment to breathe the wonderful air that's there, and it starts to shed tears."

As you can probably tell, all these explanations get jumbled up at a very early point with mysticism, and, for some desert dwellers, with a sense of duty, as well as what came to be known as the theological concept of compunction—the stabbing, piercing sense of remorse (today, the word *compunction* has been diluted to mean something closer to a momentary regret for a relatively insignificant wrong). The theology of tears also borders on Gnosticism, since one of the results of this period of incessant crying was a *knowing,* an intense awareness of a deeper-level spiritual truth as revealed by God. Gnosticism, a belief system that was particularly troublesome to the early church, maintains in part that only those who have a secret knowledge of the divine can attain salvation. But the desert fathers and mothers generally adhered to beliefs that came to be considered orthodox, and unlike genuine Gnostics, they believed that a deeper knowledge of God—the Judeo-Christian God—was attainable by anyone who sought it. Despite

Those who sow in tears will reap with shouts of joy.

—PSALM 126:5 HCSB

the emphasis on asking for the gift and seeking the gift, nearly every teacher who supported the theology of tears warned against any attempt to force the tears to come.

But from a distance of eighteen hundred years and through the lens of rational Western thinking, we see some words that may give us pause. We're supposed to *ask* for the gift of tears? What if we're not by nature the type of person who cries? What if we're not at all inclined toward contemplation or mysticism? This is supposed to help our spiritual growth—how?

And how on earth could a person cry for *days*? Many of us have known a grief so deep that it seemed as if all we could do was cry for days on end, but in reality, what we experienced were intermittent periods of weeping. The desert dwellers spoke and wrote of tears that did not stop, tears prompted by an inner weeping so complete, so all-encompassing that the outpouring seemed limitless. (Did I mention that in the sixth century Isaac the Syrian is said to have wept without ceasing for two *years*? So did Ignatius of Loyola, who lived much later and nowhere near an arid climate, so his weeping wasn't a purely desert thing.)

The doctrine of tears may seem extremist to us, but maybe we just need to examine it from a different perspective. Maybe, in placing rightful emphasis on the grace of God, we've unwittingly limited his transforming activity in our lives. Let's say God has shown me that I'm still too controlling—something so outlandish, of course, that never in a million

> *There is a sacredness in tears. They are not the mark of weakness, but of power. They speak more eloquently than ten thousand tongues. They are the messengers of overwhelming grief, of deep contrition, and of unspeakable love.*
>
> —WASHINGTON IRVING

EVAGRIUS THE INTELLECTUAL

Though the desert dwellers appear to be a wild and woolly lot, they weren't necessarily the kind of fanatics you may imagine them to be. Evagrius was among the exceptions; he was a well-educated and highly respected fourth-century church leader known for successfully debating outspoken heretics. When his bishop and mentor, Basil of Caesarea, suddenly died, the course of Evagrius's life, which seemed anchored to the church, began to take a different direction. He left Caesarea for Constantinople, where he served as a deacon under Archbishop Gregory. But after an encounter with a married woman whose husband intended revenge, Evagrius fled to Jerusalem and later the desert in Egypt. In Egypt he lived the life of an ascetic, praying, working, reading the Bible, growing his own food, and striving for a purified heart and life.

What sets Evagrius apart from many other desert fathers is the written record of his teachings. He attracted a wide following, primarily people who sought him out for spiritual direction. Among his disciples was John Cassian, something of a desert journalist who roamed throughout Egypt interviewing ascetics and later compiling their stories into a popular book. Together Evagrius and John are credited with developing an intellectual brand of desert monasticism.

Considered one of the most significant writers of his time, Evagrius became known as the father of monastic mysticism. His influence on later writers and monastics was evident long after his death. Experts who know such things say his writings, some of which have survived in remarkably good shape, indicate his familiarity with classical literature. Though his learning may have helped his credibility and authority, Evagrius apparently placed little stock in his academic background, focusing his life on the spiritual disciplines that he felt he needed to practice in order to bring his passions—which seemed to be particularly troublesome to him—under control.

years would he and I be dealing with this. I'm just hypothesizing. Anyway, I figure this is what we'll be working on for a while, and I draw on his grace for the power to mend my evil ways.

All I've done, though—and here, I do think Evagrius would agree—is allow God to crack my controlling nature, not bring me to a place of utter brokenness over the pride that lingers deep within, blocking his true lordship in my life. In essence, I've granted him permission, first, to expose one of the outward manifestations of the root sin, and second, to give me the grace to work on eliminating that outward manifestation. My attitude becomes one of "Thanks—I'll take it from here." It's a whole lot easier to draw up a list of superficial negative behaviors and clean them up than it is to cleanse my inherent sinfulness in tears of purification.

So I have asked for the gift of tears, to purify my heart and allow the light of God to shine once again in those dark areas that I wish I could keep hidden from him. Desert dwellers like Evagrius have convinced me that by watering those parched and barren areas of my life I can have the hope of seeing new life spring up in their place. If it takes tears to accomplish that, let them come in abundance.

What soap is for the body, tears are for the soul.

—JEWISH PROVERB

Chapter 2

The Jesus Prayer

Also known as a breath prayer or prayer of the heart, this tradition has gained a measure of recognition in recent decades, though not all who practice it are aware of its long history or its many functions throughout history. The simple prayer—"Lord Jesus Christ, Son of God, have mercy on me, a sinner" (some versions omit "a sinner")—sounds much too self-abasing for many Christians today, but once you give the ancients a hearing on this, you are likely to see the prayer from a far more gracious perspective.

First, a disclaimer on behalf of Christian ascetics, contemplatives, mystics, wanderers, and such throughout history: the Jesus Prayer contains no magical powers. It's not a formula that will immediately usher a person into the presence of God. The ancients knew better than that, and anyone who ascribes some kind of supernatural element to this sequence of words is not adhering to the teaching of the early Christians.

The only power, they would say with regard to this prayer, is in the name of Jesus—the name that is above all names. They called on his name with great frequency, acknowledging his lordship, reverencing him as the long-awaited Messiah, and recognizing his divinity and his relationship to God the Father in the carefully chosen words of the first half of the prayer: "Lord Jesus Christ, Son of God."

No problem so far. But then we come to "have mercy on me," which in its literal meaning should not be so problematic. How many of us, though, have heard that phrase delivered in a way that was melodramatic, sarcastic, humorous, or even mocking? Most of us, I would guess. Which is sad, given the profound truth of God's mercy. Do I want God to have mercy on me—to extend to me his eternal kindness and forgiveness and leniency? You bet I do. I'm thinking you want the same from him. It's worth getting over our cultural associations with the phrase so we can begin to plumb the depths of its truth.

Now to that dreaded word *sinner.* Again, the ancients would have had a different take on that word entirely. One of the most bewildering and disturbing discoveries in the life of the early church was the reality of postbaptismal sin. Many Christians believed that in cleansing them from sin, baptism would automatically transfer to them the power to live a sinless life. That may seem amusing to us today, but this was a serious issue for early Christians. Eventually, the church reached the consensus that

Those brought up in the tradition of the Jesus Prayer are never allowed for one moment to forget the Incarnate Christ.

—BISHOP KALLISTOS WARE

although Christ's sacrificial, redemptive death on the cross forgave us for our past, present, and future sins, the truth was that we would continue to sin throughout our lives. Using the word *sinner* in the Jesus Prayer was likely an acknowledgment of that consensus as well as a reminder of the poverty of spirit that we all experience apart from God's mercy.

To the desert dwellers and those who have discovered the value of the Jesus Prayer down through the centuries, its words summarize the essence of the gospel.

Ironically, though the first recorded reference to the Jesus Prayer dates back the sixth century, it wasn't until the first half of the twentieth that we in the West became familiar with it—and that only through the writings of an anonymous nineteenth-century Russian peasant. The now-classic book *The Way of a Pilgrim* chronicles his quest to understand what it means to pray without ceasing. He found his answer in the Jesus Prayer, which his spiritual director suggested he recite three thousand times a day, later increasing the number to twelve thousand times a day.

"Early one morning the Prayer woke me up, as it were," the Pilgrim wrote. "I started to say my usual morning prayers, but my tongue refused to say them easily or exactly. My whole desire was fixed upon one thing only—to say the Prayer of Jesus, and as soon as I went on with it I was filled with joy and relief. It was as though my lips and my tongue pronounced the words entirely of themselves without any urging from me. I spent the whole day in a state of the greatest contentment." He asked his spiritual director if

---

But the tax collector stood at a distance. He would not even look up to heaven, but beat his breast and said, "God, have mercy on me, a sinner."

—LUKE 18:13 NIV

he could recite the prayer even more frequently. (He kept track, by the way, using a special knotted rope.)

Like the ancient desert dwellers, the Pilgrim cultivated the habit of mentally praying "Lord Jesus Christ" each time he inhaled and "Have mercy on me [a sinner]" each time he exhaled. The prayer became linked with his breathing, the only thing he actually had to continue doing as he prayed—hence its designation as a breath prayer. Eventually, the prayer became so much a part of him that it became embedded in his heart; he was no longer conscious of the fact that he was praying it. No matter what else he was doing, including sleeping, his heart continued its prayer to Jesus—hence its designation as a prayer of the heart. As a result, the Pilgrim's awareness of creation and humanity intensified, and a love for both consumed him.

Neither our peasant friend nor the ancient ascetics considered this to be the only way to pray. But it served several valuable and distinct purposes for them, as it can for us today. The first is what the peasant realized, that reciting specific, prayerful words from memory opened his heart and his mind to the practice of unceasing prayer. We'll look at that in a separate reflection later on.

When the bitter cold pierces me, I begin to say my Prayer more earnestly, and I quickly become warm all over. When hunger begins to overcome me, I call more often on the Name of Jesus, and I forget my wish for food. When I fall ill and get rheumatism in my back and legs, I fix my thoughts on the Prayer, and do not notice the pain. . . . I thank God that I now understand the meaning of those words I heard in the Epistle—"Pray without ceasing."

—FROM *THE WAY OF A PILGRIM*

CAN'T DO IT?

Some people have found it helpful to mentally recite the Jesus Prayer for incrementally longer periods of time, starting with five minutes and working their way up to twenty or more. That seems to help those who can't seem to stick with the practice; the problem is often trying too hard and for too long a period of time at first. Reciting the prayer in time with rhythmic breathing helps considerably.

Like many of our ancestors and contemporaries in the faith, the ancients viewed all of life as a prayer to God. To them, praying was as natural as, well, breathing. When we get to a point where we begin to recognize the sacredness of every aspect of our lives, a simple act like praying the Jesus Prayer becomes a holy practice.

The Pilgrim's knotted rope, which helped him keep track of the number of times he recited the Jesus Prayer, is also based on an ancient tradition, one that also serves as the basis for the rosary. It's not known for certain when or where the practice began, but we know it predates Christianity and was used by practitioners of other faiths who also placed a high value on repetitious, meditative prayer.

The number of required or recommended repetitions varied from one faith to another and from one religious subgroup (such as a monastic order) to another within the same faith. Plus, differing numbers of repetitions were assigned to different purposes.

Frankly, I don't want anyone but God telling me I have to say a prescribed number of repetitive prayers, and I'm guessing many other

Then know this, you and all the people of Israel: It is by the
name of Jesus Christ of Nazareth, whom you crucified
but whom God raised from the dead,
that this man stands before you healed.

—ACTS 4:10 NIV

Christians feel the same way. But I do think there may be some lingering value in using a prayer rope or bead string or similar tool when we choose to engage in repetitive prayer, and that's to help us focus. It also brings one more sense—the sense of touch—into the prayer experience, which is why it's important to use a prayer string that feels right to you. Over the course of history, knotted ropes (and even knotted vines or other materials) were replaced by strung beads, stones, bone chips, or round berries, depending on the culture, the availability of appropriate materials, and the financial condition of the supplicant.

Strings of meditation beads (rosaries) are a more specialized form of prayer beads, and even though some Christians are now using them with greater frequency, I haven't used one enough to speak from experience. Then too, some groups are so new to this that with every source on praying the rosary you're likely to find different instructions on how to do it, which is no doubt why I gave up trying. It's also apparently a distinctly American trend within the worldwide Anglican Communion, which I discovered on a visit to Canterbury Cathedral. In that winsome way Brits have, the gift shop proprietor informed me that the only Anglicans who seemed ever to use such a thing were Americans. "It's unheard of here," she said, clearly communicating that if she had anything to do with it, the practice would remain unheard of among the rest of the Anglican Communion. I left England and made my own rosary once I got home. It rests on my dresser to this day, awaiting that so-far elusive moment when I figure out how to use it.

> *When you don't see Jesus for exactly what he was,*
> *you miss the whole point of the Jesus Prayer.*
> *If you don't understand Jesus, you can't understand his prayer—*
> *you don't get the prayer at all, you just get some kind of organized cant.*
>
> —FROM *FRANNY AND ZOOEY* BY J. D. SALINGER

For early Christians and for the Eastern Orthodox who have helped keep the Jesus Prayer alive, rhythmic breathing was and is important in their verbal communication with God. As a result, steady, concentrated breathing usually accompanies the uttering of the Jesus Prayer, which brings you into a more relaxed state and therefore a state in which you are more receptive to the work of the Spirit in your life. Unlike other forms of meditation, secular or non-Christian, deeper relaxation is not the goal but a natural consequence of this type of prayer. Silence helps immensely, but even without it you can reach a point of stillness and focus, a point where you've cleared away the clutter and where God can have unimpeded access to do the work he wants to do in your life.

Some people, myself included, have found the Jesus Prayer to be helpful in corralling wandering minds during times of intentional prayer. Repeating those words helps me to re-collect my thoughts and refocus my heart and mind on God. I've also found it helpful anytime my thoughts wander when I'd prefer that they didn't, like in the many periods of silence between the various elements in the five daily prayer services at the Benedictine monastery I occasionally visit. And it's regularly used by many people as they take walks or jog or do any kind of repetitious exercise.

Is there any biblical basis for the Jesus Prayer? I wondered that myself and discovered that there very well may be a more direct basis than I understood. Breath prayer was apparently associated with the Psalms and was practiced at first by the Jews. Some scholars of early Christian

In that day you will no longer ask me anything. I tell you the truth, my Father will give you whatever you ask in my name. Until now you have not asked for anything in my name. Ask and you will receive, and your joy will be complete.

—JOHN 16:23–24 NIV

writings believe the desert dwellers based the prayer on Paul's assertion in 1 Corinthians 14:19 that "in the church I would rather speak five words with my understanding, that I may teach others also, than ten thousand words in a tongue" (NKJV). In Greek and in our peasant friend's native Russian, the Jesus Prayer is expressed in five words. Or so I'm told.

In any event, it's not the exact words of the prayer but the intent of the prayer that matters. What is crucial is that in any short, meditative, and repetitive utterance, the name of Jesus remains central. For me, the Jesus Prayer accomplishes that, though I confess that my Boomer sensibilities compel me to customize it: "Lord Jesus Christ, Son of God, have mercy on me, a sinner . . . saved by grace." It's not metrically correct, but it suits me much better—ending not on a sin note but on a grace note.

Keep watch in your heart; and with watchfulness say in your mind with awe and trembling: "Lord Jesus Christ, have mercy upon me."

—PHILIMON, SIXTH-CENTURY EGYPTIAN MONK

Chapter 3

A Time to Grieve

For all our sophistication, all our knowledge, all our understanding of psychology, we in America are often clueless when it comes to grieving. At least that seems to be the case in "assimilated" America, more so than in segments of our culture where there's a solid ethnic identification. Except for the lucky few who have a strong sense of heritage, most of us don't know how to mourn in a way that won't come back to bite us later on. We allow ourselves three days of bereavement and no more, unless the situation is particularly tragic. We suppress the pain or anesthetize it in questionable ways, and think we've dealt with it. We haven't.

Long before the advent of Christianity, the Jews established a pattern of dealing with death that has survived at least four millennia. Joseph—yes, the Joseph of Genesis—became the model for the Israelites' handling of grief when he set aside a full seven days to mourn the loss of his father Jacob (Gen. 50:10). You may recognize this as the forerunner of the contemporary Jewish practice of sitting shivah—a week-long period of bereavement that not only allows the family and loved ones to properly grieve but also forces the outside world to realize that something is amiss.

During shivah, the family ceases all unnecessary activity. Their world essentially stops as they acclimate to a life without their loved one. They are not to cook or clean or carry out any similar routine tasks. (For a long time, bathing was not even permitted, though that restriction has been relaxed. Now, you can get clean, as long as you don't indulge in a bubble bath or spa or the like.) In the Middle Ages, mirrors were covered to keep the soul from seeing its reflection; that superstition is gone, but mirrors may still be covered to remind the mourners that appearances are not important at this time.

In rabbinical tradition, sitting shivah is a gift, not an obligation, and surviving family members are permitted to return to work in three days, if necessary, which is likely the source of our three-day period of mourning. If that's the case—if our three days of bereavement can be traced to rabbinic writings—I have to wonder what our culture of grief would look like had the full seven days of mourning been considered a requirement. I'm sure I would have been the first to complain about the legalism, but there's something to be said here in favor of forced inactivity. It's hard to imagine an employer today allowing a week off for the death of a family member (depending on the circumstances, that is), but had it been the

No one ever told me that grief felt so like fear.

—C. S. LEWIS

norm for millennia, it's possible that a full week off would have survived as a standard practice even today.

Ideally, as a family is sitting shivah, there is to be no superficial conversation. The grieving family is not even to ask about the welfare of the guests who come to express their condolences or mourn with them. There is to be no focus on the self, neither on the part of the family nor on the part of the guests. Having been through the discomfort of hearing a woman complain about her cheating husband to my grieving mother—who at that moment just wanted her own husband back—I hereby call for an immediate return to this tradition. The sooner, the better. Today would be good.

The Hebrew Scriptures (what we call the Old Testament) provide insight into a separate tradition that is being revived among present-day Jews as well as Gentiles, the practice of preparing an "ethical will." That description is a bit misleading, implying that any other wills are unethical. The term refers to the legacy the deceased has left behind and the particular blessings he or she wished to impart to the survivors. If you're familiar with the story of Jacob, you recall the deathbed scene in the latter chapters of Genesis in which he blesses his children and grandchildren and shares with them insights God has given him about their future. That story and others like it set the precedent for leaving an ethical will, a document that can include such diverse elements as spiritual lessons and burial instructions.

The ancient ritual of rending one's garment is another aspect of bereavement that has survived among Jews into the twenty-first century. Upon first learning of the death of a loved one, a survivor tears whatever

I am weary from grief;
strengthen me through Your word.

—PSALM 119:28 HCSB

he or she is wearing. You see this throughout the Hebrew Scriptures, even when the grief stems not from the death of a loved one but from Israel's turning away from God once again. Though the practice continues today, now it's often a more symbolic "rending" of a black ribbon or a small tear made in a piece of fabric. Ironic, when you consider that an ancient Israelite may have torn his only robe in despair, while most of us today can readily replace the clothes we're wearing.

As for me, I'd like to go back to the whole rending thing. It sure beats breaking a window or kicking my foot through a wall, which is what I felt like doing when I found out that a close friend had been killed in a car crash in the summer of 1970. I had just turned 20, and being a WASP with neither an ethnic tradition nor a faith tradition at the time, I handled the grief poorly—so poorly that I have no memory of the three days between the accident and the graveside service. The day after the funeral I returned to work, nowhere near to being equipped to get on with normal living after suffering the greatest loss of my life to that point. No one knew how to equip me, it seemed, and I sure couldn't do it myself.

Part of the rending ritual I could have used most back then was the accompanying lament: *barukh atah adonai elohenu melekh ha-olam dayyan ha-'emet*—"Blessed is God, ruler of the universe, the just judge." The idea is that God, who determines the length of a person's life, is just and knows what he is doing, even if we don't. I certainly didn't know, and at the time,

---

We dare not steel ourselves against our trials, running away from the
fires where our pruned branches crumble to ashes.
For if we escape those flames,
we will risk barrenness of soul and will miss out on the beauty
that only is born through the ashes of yesterday's grief.

—CAMMIE VAN ROOY

my complicated but naïve theology left me bereft of any consolation what-soever. My friend was gone, and the future was bleak and unfathomable. Very Camus, very Sartre, very depressing indeed. There was no one to share my grief, unless I count one guy who thought we should mourn by getting cozy. I declined.

According to the ancient tradition, the mourner would rend his or her garment while simultaneously crying out the "blessed is God" response. But there's more: The one who discovers the body of the deceased is respon-sible for closing the eyes and mouth on the body, covering the entire body with a sheet—and guarding over the body until the burial, reciting psalms all the while. Aside from the temptation to quickly leave the room that I suspect would overcome many Americans, there's an obvious reason why this ritual is frowned upon today, what with hospital staff and coroners and funeral directors laying their claim on the body at appointed times throughout the postmortem period. But I think there's something to be said here for practicing as much of the ritual as possible.

As with any meaningful ritual, this one serves a much-needed and distinct purpose, which is to ground the mourner and allow her to collect her thoughts and emotions at a time of intense confusion and bewilderment. Recitation of the psalms has long been considered a valuable meditative activity, so much so that until recent history, it was not unusual to find

> *Then the virgin will rejoice with dancing,*
> *while young and old men {rejoice} together.*
> *I will turn their mourning into joy,*
> *give them consolation,*
> *and {bring} happiness out of grief.*
>
> —JEREMIAH 31:13 HCSB

Christians and Jews alike who had memorized all one hundred fifty bibli-cal psalms.

We've lost so much with our contemporary insistence that we "just can't memorize anything," and so our adult Christian curricula—if they advocate memorizing at all—challenge students with one memory verse per week. Granted, you could meditate on a single Bible verse for a week or a month or a lifetime and not plumb its depths, depending on the verse you choose. But we're talking about memorization, not meditation, and a generation that still remembers the lyrics to "American Pie" or a generation that can quote the entire script of *The Matrix* can be trusted to have the brain power to memorize a psalm or two.

But that's another tradition entirely.

Where grief is fresh, any attempt to divert it only irritates.

—SAMUEL JOHNSON

Chapter 4

True Silence

In some parts of the country, far from the madding crowds of my unnatural habitat near Orlando, it's still possible to experience genuine silence and live to tell about it. I know this because I did both. It happened only once, while I was house-hunting near Cody, Wyoming. As I looked over the seven acres I had hoped would soon be ours, I realized that the only sound I could hear was that of my own breathing. So I stopped breathing, just long enough to prove to myself that the silence was real. There were no sounds—no wind, no flicking grasshoppers, no ticking from the engine of my car as it cooled down. Nothing. It was glorious. And then I inhaled. Oh well.

No wonder the desert fathers and mothers in the early centuries were able to experience silence, I thought; that's all they had. Not being too swift on the uptake, at first I didn't catch God's little object lesson out there on the Wyoming desert, when my ears heard nothing but my insides were restless to stake my claim on that land. He had allowed me to experience sensory silence that day so he could prepare me for what the desert mothers and fathers really experienced, what I now call "true" silence—silence of the mind and spirit. He didn't take his time about it either, because not long after I returned home from that trip—without a desert dwelling, I might add—I had an opportunity to attend a silent retreat.

Like many first-timers, I was petrified. Not of the silence itself but of the very real possibility that I would violate the silence. I convinced myself that everyone else would know the ropes that I clearly did not know. I was certain I would do something to incur the wrath of the retreat directors, neither of whom I had ever met. The closer I came to the retreat center, the closer I came to doing a 180—turning the car around and never looking back. The bright lights of Orlando were beckoning me to return to the Land of Incessant Chatter.

I soldiered on, grimly deciding that if they treated me badly, I'd huffily tell those retreat directors that I *thought* they were *Christians! That* would silence them for *sure.* Instead, they silenced my attitude and my fears with a grace that I swear exuded from their pores. The directors turned out to be two of the most gracious people I have ever known. Just as I had suspected, the other retreatants knew the ropes, but trust me, the ropes weren't all that hard to figure out: Avoid unnecessary conversation. Speak in a low voice when you do need to say something. Respect others' need for silence.

The fewer the words, the better the prayer.

—MARTIN LUTHER

Why Silence?

I'll be the first to admit that my periods of silence are few and far between and that I have a long way to go before I can say that the lessons I've learned from silence have truly transformed my life. But I can say this without equivocation: Silence has an awesome transformative power. And I use the word *awesome* intentionally and deliberately here; our culture may carelessly throw that word around, using it to refer to everything from the latest underground band to Starbucks' latest concoction, but I'm using it right now in its literal sense of inspiring awe.

- Silence inspires awe when it causes me—me!—to stop obsessing about the unending, soul-crushing, Spirit-quenching details of my everyday life.
- Silence inspires awe when it shows me how little I listen to what people are saying to me, both in their actual words and in the real meaning behind the words they're speaking.
- Silence inspires awe when it underscores the hundreds of unnecessary words I utter each day.
- Silence inspires awe when it diverts my attention away from the chatter in my head and toward the wonder that the rest of life—the authentic life—contains.
- Silence inspires awe when it overcomes the discomfort I feel when I experience silence in the company of other people.
- Silence inspires awe when it removes my desire to talk for a few peace-filled hours.
- Silence inspires awe when it quells the very fear it provokes: the fear of silence itself, the fear that keeps me turning up the noise to ward off all the other fears that consume me.
- Silence inspires awe when it makes a place where I can hear the voice of God.

Move slowly and quietly throughout the retreat center. Pretty simple rules, really. (I was especially happy to discover that I, an admitted salt addict, was allowed to ask someone to pass it to me during meals.)

Our goal, of course, was not physical silence—the kind I experienced in the desert—but mental and spiritual silence—the kind that I had never before experienced. To support that, one of the directors softly read poetry or an appropriate portion of Scripture during our mealtimes. One poem, "A House at Rest" by Jessica Powers, was particularly instrumental in quelling the inner turmoil I had brought along with me. Though it took a full two days, by the third day I was experiencing true silence, a peacefulness that stayed with me for the remainder of the week.

That's all well and good for a retreat setting. Even though adjusting to physical silence can be a challenge, it's much easier if everyone around you cooperates because they are also trying to achieve mental and spiritual silence. But most of us can't live in a retreat setting full-time, though I'm thinking those retreat directors know a good gig when they see one. Their lives appear to be awfully attractive until you realize that they have to put up with newbies who arrive with a carload of attitude and fear and preconceived notions. Like one person I know intimately.

Is it possible to experience true silence in a noisy environment—say, the vacation capital of the world? It's not always easy, but yes, it is possible. I've done it, and once again I've lived to tell about it, mainly because I stopped bothering to hold my breath. What I do with my breath now is to

In prayer it is better to have a heart without words
than words without a heart.

—JOHN BUNYAN

inhale deeply. Once, twice, as many times as it takes to consciously reverse the habit of shallow breathing. And exhale, of course.

I also make sure I'm in what is laughingly called a "comfortable position," which in this context is definitely a relative phrase. Comfortable to me means lying in a hammock or lounging in an overstuffed recliner or stretching out on a wickedly soft sofa. But that's not how I experience true silence; that's how I experience the alternate universe that is my dream life. No, to truly *experience* silence you have to be fully engaged in the process, which for me means that I need to sit up straight. Didn't I tell you this isn't always easy? However, this is true for me: I can quiet my mind and spirit much more quickly when my body cooperates by resisting its natural tendency to slouch and loll.

Now here's the key: Next I consciously dismiss the cares of my life as irrelevant intrusions. They aren't, of course, but that's the way I get rid of them. Remember Gloria Gaynor's "I Will Survive," those of you who yourselves survived the disco era? If so, you know the lyrics I'm referring to, the ones I dare not repeat here lest ASCAP's lawyers smell copyright infringement, bringing untold grief on Broadman & Holman and all their offspring, to the third and fourth generation. Finally, I shove my cares out the door, telling them in no uncertain terms that this is *my* time, *my* silence, *my* peace and quiet.

I'm there at last. Silent mind, silent spirit, ready and willing and open to whatever God has for me, even if it appears to be nothing. Even if it's just the silence. Because true silence is never "just" silence; it's always a time of

---

Silence is praise to you, Zion-dwelling GOD. And also obedience.

—PSALM 65:1 MSG

blessing. Each period of silence, no matter how short, builds on the previous one until entering into true silence becomes almost natural. Almost.

If you've tried to experience true silence but simply haven't been able to, let go of your efforts for a while. For me, striving is always counter-productive unless I'm engaged in spiritual warfare, which I strive not to be engaged in but end up there, anyway. I ask you: What's the point of striving? Just give it up. It won't work.

Remember this: Silence is not an escape. It's a doorway into God's presence. And be prepared for this: You will become increasingly sensitive to the abundance of unnecessary talk that characterizes your daily life. You may even find yourself using fewer words. Said desert-dweller Arsenius: "I have often repented of having spoken but never of having remained silent." Amen to that.

Silence is as deep as eternity, speech as shallow as time.
—THOMAS CARLYLE

Chapter 5

Prayer Shawls

Though they're called by different names, prayer shawls have a place in many religious traditions. Among Christians, the use of shawls stems from a tradition of the ancient Hebrews, whose custom of wearing a tallit continues today among Jewish men and, in Reform congregations, women. The *tallit* serves to remind the wearer to observe Jewish law.

God laid down that law to the Israelites: "GOD spoke to Moses: 'Speak to the People of Israel. Tell them that from now on they are to make tassels on the corners of their garments and to mark each corner tassel with a blue thread. When you look at these tassels you'll remember and keep all the commandments of GOD, and not get distracted by everything you feel or see that seduces you into infidelities. The tassels will signal remembrance and observance of all my commandments, to live a holy life to GOD. I am your GOD who rescued you from the land of Egypt to be your personal God. Yes, I am GOD, your God'" (Num. 15:37–41 MSG).

The tassels on the corners of the tallit in particular are intended to remind the Israelites of the law of God. The shawls are actually long scarves—you've seen them in every movie that depicts a synagogue service, including a bar mitzvah—and not the triangular shawls that we've become accustomed to as fashion accessories for women. They always have a blue-threaded tassel on each corner.

I only recently discovered information about the contemporary use of prayer shawls among Christians. Prayer shawls are used by some Christians these days to serve as a tangible reminder of God's lovingkindness and comforting presence. When you wrap yourself in a shawl and begin to pray, you acknowledge the love of God that constantly surrounds you. I like that image, and I need that reminder. But there are more reasons to use them.

Soon after I first heard about modern use of prayer shawls, I visited a church where a pile of crocheted and knitted shawls had been placed in front of the altar. During the announcements, the pastor described the church's prayer-shawl ministry: on a regular basis, a group of women (men were invited, but . . .) would spend the day making the shawls, praying over them as they worked—praying that God would bless the unknown recipient, bringing to that person healing or comfort or whatever else might be needed. Then the shawls were brought to the church to be prayed over by the congregation before being distributed to people who were ill or grieving or despairing. Each person would have the comfort of knowing that

Become so wrapped up in something that you forget to be afraid.

—LADY BIRD JOHNSON

someone, somewhere—the woman who created the shawl—was continuing to pray for him or her.

We were told of an unplanned visit to a twelve-year-old boy in the hospital suffering from cancer. The boy was propped up, the shawl draped around his shoulders. He told the minister that he removed it only to sleep. It had become a symbol of both God's love and the kindness of people.

After hearing that story, I had to find out more about prayer shawls. So I went to my favorite research assistant, Google, and discovered a fair amount of information on the Internet about prayer-shawl ministries. And I learned that in some mainline denominational churches—lo and behold!—not only were men wearing the shawls, they were also helping to make them.

On some of the Web sites, people posted stories about how the shawls had ministered to different people. One woman put on her shawl when she woke up in the middle of the night, alone and afraid; another woman wore hers before and after her mastectomy as a reminder of the prayers and support of her friends. A man diagnosed with terminal lung cancer watched as his daughter knitted a shawl for him; he wore it until the day of his death—and beyond. Just before the casket was closed for the final time, his daughter draped his body with his beloved prayer shawl.

People suffering from debilitating chronic depression, a man with Alzheimer's, a woman entering seminary late in life, a wife and mother of three children whose husband was serving in Iraq—their stories just about moved me to tears, which doesn't happen very often to me.

A homemade friend wears longer than one you buy in the market.
—AUSTIN O'MALLEY

And then there were the stories told by the knitters themselves. Lots of women knit prayer shawls on their own, but many join knitting circles like the one at the church I visited. If you just got an image of a group of elderly women sitting around knitting because they're the ones with the spare time to engage in that kind of hobby, let me dispel you of that notion on three counts. One, shawl-knitting ministries attract women (and the occasional man) from all walks of life and from all age groups—even teens and children. Two, this is no hobby; they'll tell you in no uncertain terms that knitting prayer shawls is a ministry and that the knitting itself is a meditative, spiritual activity. And three, older women these days, at least the ones I know and the ones likely to get involved in this kind of ministry, hardly have the spare time we once associated with retirement.

But back to the knitting circles. Some, I'm sure, are socially oriented, like the quilting bees of old that gave women an opportunity to visit with one another while at the same time being productive. Other groups, though, give precedence to the ministry aspect. Some groups spend the first hour or so in complete silence. Women filter in, join the circle, and begin knitting. After the time of silence, they begin to share their concerns about the people they're knitting for, or update the group on a situation they discussed in a previous meeting, or seek and give help on knitting problems.

> *If we are indeed made in the image of our Creator, it stands to reason that we are most like that Creator when we are creating something ourselves.*
> *So the very act is sacred, from the most humbling piecing of fabric to the soaring stonework of the great Gothic cathedrals. . . .*
> *The making of cloth or other objects needed for everyday life lends itself naturally to ritual, and ritual also is basic to human life.*
> —SUSAN GORDON LYDON

That hour of silence serves many purposes. It enables the knitters to privately unload all the petty concerns they've brought with them—the traffic, the weather, the last-minute minicrises that threatened to sabotage their efforts to get to the meeting. It gives them an opportunity to settle their minds and their spirits and enter into the rhythm of the knitting circle. And it provides a time for silent prayer and meditation. By the time they begin to talk again, deeper issues have risen to the surface. The silence has had a calming effect, and the knitters share their concerns with one another in a more thoughtful and reflective manner. Prayer flows in and out of their conversation, and the experience of knitting becomes a fully spiritual one. There is a social element to their time together, but the faith element envelops it.

As I read about knitting and prayer shawl ministries, I began to discover a number of metaphors that applied to the spiritual life—and I took up knitting again after a thirty-year break. It took no time at all for me to grasp the relevance of Paul's observation in Ephesians that as Christians we are "knit together in love" or how Jonathan's soul was knit to David's. As I began creating a prayer shawl for a friend whose husband had recently died, and as I prayed over nearly every stitch, I felt knit to her in a way I had never experienced before.

Then there's the whole lesson about accepting our imperfections because we are an imperfect people. In many faith traditions, artisans intentionally make a mistake in every piece they work on as a way of honoring the perfection of God. Christianity is no exception; whether the piece is a

---

Knitting reminds me of certain religious truths which seem to show up in most religious traditions. For example, you can rip it out and start over, if need be. There is always another chance.

—BETTY BERLENBACH, A KNITTING PASTOR

handmade vestment, an illuminated manuscript, or a hand-thrown pottery chalice to be used for the Eucharist, a tiny flaw will be left in or on the item as a reminder of our humanity and God's perfection. I've been blessed with never having to intentionally insert a flaw since making mistakes comes so naturally to me. I have, though, learned to be a bit more forgiving and a lot less impatient when I do make mistakes, whether it's in the shawl I'm knitting or the life I'm living.

Long before I started knitting again and began making shawls for other people, I naturally decided that I had to have a prayer shawl of my own. Not one to be content with something I already had on hand, I embarked on a quest for the perfect shawl. I tell you, nothing can tank a spiritual exercise faster than the need to have *just the right item* in order to begin practicing it. It's like when I took up jogging back in the 1970s. Shorts and a T-shirt would not do; I had to have a jogging suit, which I was convinced would help me run better and longer. It didn't, but at the time I probably would have argued that it very well did.

Fortunately, my sane and sensitive friend Rae—may her sane and sensitive tribe increase!—intervened. After I mentioned the whole prayer-shawl thing to her, and while I was obsessing over the kind of shawl I should buy, Rae actually *prayed* about it and decided to send me a shawl that had special meaning for her. Now I fully understand how all those shawl recipients feel. When I place that shawl around me, it's as if Rae is hugging me. We haven't seen each other in something like twenty years,

Friends show their love in times of trouble.

—EURIPIDES

but her gift envelops me in her presence and in the presence of God. What a treasure that is.

Do I use mine each time I pray? No, most likely because I'm doing good to simply *remember* to pray, never mind thinking about my wardrobe at the same time. But I do use it from time to time, and I take it with me when I travel.

Like other tangible objects the ancients used in worship, there's no magical power or superstitious element associated with prayer shawls. But what a loving reminder they are of God! And when they're received as a gift, that loving reminder extends to the giver.

> *They were all dressed in elegant linen—David, the Levites carrying the Chest, the choir and band, and Kenaniah who was directing the music. David also wore a linen prayer shawl (called an ephod).*
>
> —1 CHRONICLES 15:27 MSG

Chapter 6

Spiritual Solitude

R emember Antony, the Egyptian who is considered to be the first monk in history? The one who did a whole lot of things that seem bizarre to us today, like praying for days while standing in the shape of a cross? I mentioned him in the introduction, which I cleverly titled "Beginnings" so you might actually read it. Well, Antony, who was born in the middle of the third century and lived for more than a hundred years, was by all accounts a mentally stable, kind, and compassionate man. But that stability, kindness, and compassion came at a cost—twenty years of living in solitude in the desert.

For Antony, there was no other way to confront his demons. He fled society, but only because he knew the lure of the world would distract him from the hard work ahead. Christ was his all, and he wanted Christ to consume him. Until he vanquished his enemies—his anger, his selfishness, his sinful nature—that could not happen. Instead of escaping from reality, he faced it head on in the isolation of the desert, often in the form of demons that left him bloody and scarred.

I'm guessing here, but I doubt Antony expected this to take twenty years. From what is known of him, he had no fixed expectations when he set out for the desert. But he ended up engaged in a series of demonic battles that would have sent most of us hightailing it for the nearest outpost of civilization, even if it meant swimming the croc-infested Nile to get there.

What Antony experienced in his time of solitude was the transforming fire of purification, which Henri Nouwen has called "the furnace of transformation." Solitude, as it turns out, tends to burn the old self right up.

Along about now, you've got to be wondering if I've taken leave of my senses. Spend twenty years in solitude? Be purified by fire? Enter the furnace of transformation? Um, can't we just let the old self die of natural causes after it reaches a ripe old age?

Well, sure we can. But stay with me here and look at what Nouwen has written next: "Without solitude we remain victims of our society and continue to be entangled in the illusions of the false self." (He wrote this in 1981, before "victim" was a whiny word.) Even short periods of solitude bring us face-to-face with what we've become: a product of our culture and a stranger to the person we started out to be. Like Antony, we are so

Now in the morning, having risen a long while before daylight,
He went out and departed to a solitary place; and there He prayed.

—MARK 1:35 NKJV

immersed in society that we cannot easily separate ourselves from its influ-ence. Our very personalities, as well as our habits and the other norms of our lives, have been shaped in large part by that society. Only by consciously detaching and spending time in solitude can we ever hope to rediscover our *real* self, the person we are, at the core of our being.

But what exactly is solitude—that is, solitude as a spiritual exercise? I can tell you what it's not: it's not simply being alone, basking in some much-needed private time. It's not a luxuriously long bubble bath or a stolen hour away from the rest of the household. And it's not what we typi-cally think of as a retreat, especially a group retreat. It's an intense time of isolation from the world and its control.

So here's what you'll need to take along with you in order to experi-ence life-transforming solitude: nothing. Absolutely nothing. And that includes your Bible.

Before you cry "Heretic!" hear me out. Allowing God to change us in the fire of purification is one of the hardest things we'll ever do. Imagine standing in front of a flame-filled furnace and hearing God tell you to enter. Now I don't know about you, but I'd use every spiritual trick in the book to avoid crossing *that* threshold. "Hold it, God. I haven't had my devotions today," I'd be tempted to say. "I'll be right with you, once I read Ezekiel and maybe a dozen or so psalms, and, oh, I forgot my reading from the Gospels today! I'll even read it out loud to you, nice and slow-like." Maybe you've never used Bible reading as a stalling tactic, but I've mastered the fine art of postponing transformation through scriptural recitation.

> *Our language has wisely sensed the two sides of being alone.*
> *It has created the word loneliness to express the pain of being alone.*
> *And it has created the word solitude to express the glory of being alone.*
> —PAUL TILLICH

A Healthy Re-entry

One of the dangers of prolonged or frequent periods of solitude is the temptation to withdraw so far into yourself that you run the risk of forgetting all about that big old world out there. Not literally, of course. But it is possible to find so much pleasure in your time alone with God, and to become so focused on the transformation that's taking place in your life, that you want to shut out the world and live in the solitude that you've come to love. While you may not be tempted to live like a hermit, you may be tempted to live inside your own head a bit too much.

A strong indication that your time alone has truly been time spent with God is the increased compassion you have toward others when you reenter the world. You will likely see more clearly the loneliness of so many people despite their crowded, busy lives; you may also become acutely aware of the emotional and physical pain and suffering in their lives as well. But you are also likely to find joy and wonder in the most ordinary things.

If solitude is beginning to sound more like torture and less like blessing, you're beginning to get the hang of it. I like being alone, but the kind of solitude I'm describing is another matter. It's not as if I wake up on a Friday morning and cheerily announce, "I think I'll go find that furnace of transformation this weekend!" No, I know what I'm getting into when I schedule time alone at a prayer center or monastery or convent. Those

The wilderness and the solitary place shall be glad for them; and the desert shall rejoice, and blossom as the rose.

—ISAIAH 35:1 KJV

By withdrawing from others and paring your life down to the bare essentials for even a short amount of time, you give your senses an opportunity to become refreshed. Your senses come back to life when you once again surround yourself with people and sights and sounds and smells, to the point where it may feel overwhelming. Returning from solitude can be bittersweet, but then that's the case at any time we return to our ordinary lives following an extraordinary experience.

And then there's the problem of loneliness. Times of solitude can make you realize how very lonely you are in your real life, the one that's filled with people and activities and way too much stuff. Trying to combat that loneliness is pretty much a losing battle. I am convinced that loneliness is our natural state, the reality of our lives apart from the immediate and eternal presence of God. That shouldn't be a depressing thought. It should make us accept our loneliness, empathize with others in their loneliness, and together look forward to the day when we will be ushered into God's immediate and eternal presence.

Until then, we have our times of solitude, however rare, to look forward to.

are the only places where I've been able to experience genuine solitude, the kind that says to God, "Okay, come and get me. I'm all yours. Do with me what you will."

Then he does with me what he will, and it's no fun.

But I have to keep remembering that fun is not what I signed on for. When I came to faith in Christ, I was so broken that I had no hope that

One must learn an inner solitude, where or with whomsoever he may be.
He must learn to penetrate things and find God there,
to get a strong impression of God firmly fixed on his mind.

—MEISTER ECKHART

he could or would fix me. I didn't come to him to be fixed; I came to him hoping that maybe he could just hold the shards of my life in his hands for awhile, even if he couldn't put them back together again and make me whole. My life no longer mattered to me.

Christ was my all, and I wanted Christ to consume me.

But I did not flee to the desert like Antony. I became a "victim" of my society—which, by the way, includes the church—and continued to be entangled in the illusions of my false self. I conveniently forgot that my passion as a new believer was to become like Christ. Instead, I became like . . . well, everybody else.

Solitude gives me an opportunity to continue to get to know myself, my real self, the person I was meant to be all along. More importantly, it gives God an unimpeded opportunity to transform me, because I enter solitude unwilling to resist him any longer.

If it means being consumed by Christ, I welcome the fire.

Now when Jesus heard this, he withdrew from there in a boat to a lonely place apart. But when the crowds heard it, they followed him on foot from the towns.

—MATTHEW 14:13 RSV

Chapter 7

Contemplative Prayer

S ay the word *contemplation* around some people and the image of a navel immediately pops up in their heads. Sitting and contemplating that weird curlicue at the center of their torsos is what they've come to imagine contemplation to be.

Other equally distorted views of contemplation have prevailed at different times and in different cultures down through the centuries, often creating the mistaken impression that only mystics or saints or creepy, otherworldly hermits are able to engage in the practice. Well, I'm no mystic or saint or otherworldly hermit—creepy or otherwise—and I've practiced contemplation, in the form of contemplative prayer. Once in a while. Which rules me out as a true contemplative, but we'll get to that in a minute. Meantime, rest assured that my navel never figures into my prayer time.

As you probably suspect, contemplative prayer is silent prayer. It's distinctive from meditation in that in contemplative prayer the mind is disengaged, as much as is possible. In meditation, the mind remains active, reflecting on God or Scripture or another element of the faith. I like James Borst's simple definition of contemplation: "There is a simple gazing (looking) at the Lord while the heart reaches out in wordless prayer and the will seeks to be one with his." Borst compares meditation to painting a picture and contemplation to looking at the completed painting.

With contemplative prayer, your spirit is fully open to God's Spirit. For an hour. A whole hour. I'm not kidding. At *least* an hour, in fact, if you're me. It takes that long for me to settle down my restless nature and have any hope of achieving contemplation.

The ancients, especially the desert dwellers, often prayed much longer than an hour, not having wristwatch-wearing bosses or soccer-practicing kids or schedule-robbing ministries or anything like that. No, they could pray for *days* and their world wouldn't fall apart.

Not so for us. About the only time we could hope to find more than an hour for contemplative prayer is while we're on retreat. And I don't mean a church retreat or a "preached" retreat, the kind where you listen to a speaker, spend time reflecting on the message (or—ugh!—filling in the blanks in a workbook), and then reassemble to share your thoughts with others. Those kinds of retreats offer precious little time to hear yourself think, let alone to truly retreat. No, I mean a personal retreat of several days or more at a place supportive of your need to be alone—a monastery,

Pray especially for rulers and their governments to rule well so we can be quietly about our business of living simply, in humble contemplation.

—1 TIMOTHY 2:2 MSG

convent, prayer center, or a cabin in the woods, as long as it doesn't have phone service or television reception of any kind.

But back to that hour. There's a reason why an hour is considered the baseline for experiencing true contemplative prayer. Those who regularly practice contemplative prayer attest to the fact that you spend a fair amount of time unloading at the beginning of the hour—quieting your spirit, quelling your impulses, ridding your mind of "vain imaginings," and bringing your heart under control. If you stop before accomplishing all that, you've wasted your time because you haven't reached a state of true contemplation. That's why contemplatives pretty much insist on a full hour; less than that means you've probably spent very little time in genuine contemplation.

Let me tell you, sitting in silence for a full hour can be agonizing. The first few times you attempt it, your body will start fidgeting and your mind will start wandering well before the five-minute mark. At ten minutes, you'll feel like jumping out of your skin; at fifteen you'll become convinced that the clock has stopped; at twenty—should you even make it that far the first time out—you'll make the appointment for a root canal that you've been putting off because you know it can't be any worse than this.

No doubt about it: you have to have a powerful attraction to this exercise to practice it. Some would say you have to be called.

Which is probably one reason why I am not a true contemplative. The other reason is that while anyone can practice contemplative prayer,

---

Those who are more adapted to the active life can prepare themselves for contemplation in the practice of the active life, while those who are more adapted to the contemplative life can take upon themselves the works of the active life so as to become yet more apt for contemplation.

—THOMAS AQUINAS

a true contemplative practices daily. For such a person, the desire for God expressed through contemplative prayer is so deep that he or she would not consider allowing a day to go by without engaging in the practice.

The anonymous author of a fifteenth-century manuscript, *The Cloud of Unknowing,* wrote that when the practice of contemplation seizes you, "it will follow you to bed at night and rise with you in the morning. It will pursue you through the day in everything you do, intruding into your usual daily devotions like a barrier between you and them."

Let's assume for the moment that you just want to try this out. You haven't heard "the call," if there even is such a thing, but there's something here that appeals to you. Maybe it's simply this: unlike spoken prayers uttered in the midst of crisis or turmoil or desperate need, contemplative prayer brings us to a place of rest in the Lord's presence. There's no intensity or anxiety involved; we don't need to work hard at concentrating on this or that aspect of God or expend enormous effort trying to attain some mystical state. We just need to gently release everything into God's loving care and trust him to help us through this spiritual exercise.

By now you know the drill for many similar exercises. Sit comfortably but with your spine straight to help maintain alertness. Breathe deeply and rhythmically, holding your breath briefly after each inhalation and exhalation; this relaxes you and keeps your mind and senses occupied while your spirit settles down. Fix your eyes on something straight ahead—perhaps an object that reminds you of God, though an imaginary point on the wall will work just as well. Don't allow your eyes to wander, because your mind

God, within Your temple,
we contemplate Your faithful love.

—Psalm 48:9 HCSB

can't help but follow. I suggest placing a non-ticking clock just at the edge of your peripheral vision. Glance at it occasionally when you feel you need to, but immediately return your gaze to the original fixed point.

Anytime your mind wanders, mentally and repetitiously recite the Jesus Prayer (see chapter 2), a short phrase from the Lord's Prayer, like "Our Father, which art in heaven, hallowed be thy name," or another prayerful phrase that's meaningful to you. You'll soon become consciously aware of God's presence surrounding you.

What happens next for many people is that in their complete openness and surrender to God, as well as in their unquestioned acceptance of his will, they see more clearly than ever the sin that separates them from God. That doesn't mean you need to examine your life at this point; that's for another time and place. What is revealed is not a catalog of individual sins but an awareness of *sin*. Once you repent and accept God's forgiveness, there are no barriers left between you and God. Your mind, your emotions, your impulses, your heart, your sin—all have been dealt with and dismissed. As *The Cloud* author wrote: "A naked intent toward God, the desire for him alone, is enough."

God responds by invading your open spirit, consuming you as you have always longed he would. You are no longer the only one doing the gazing; God is also gazing upon you. That's contemplative prayer.

As a result of all this, we cannot help but be transformed. As we practice contemplative prayer, God increases, and we decrease. All those circumstances that make us angry, fearful, possessive, bitter, suspicious,

What a man takes in by contemplation, that he pours out in love.

—MEISTER ECKHART

and so forth—the things of earth that rob us of the peace we find in God's presence—all those things "grow strangely dim, in the light of his glory and grace," as the wonderful hymn "Turn Your Eyes upon Jesus" expresses it. It's worth giving over an hour—roughly 4 percent of our day—for that alone. Once in a while, anyway—unless you're really, *really* called to be a contemplative.

> *The wicked hope to destroy me,*
> *but I contemplate Your decrees.*
>
> —PSALM 119:95 HCSB

Chapter 8

Memorial Meals

Not long ago I saw a report on the local news about a family that had invited everyone in their small community to an unusual celebration: a picnic honoring the one-year anniversary of the death of the family patriarch. The elderly man had been something of a fixture in this Southern town, sitting on a rickety chair outside his grocery store day after day, waiting for the occasional customer and waving to passersby.

His widow had been so distraught over his death that she felt she had neglected to thank the community for their support during her time of grief. This picnic—this "memorial meal," as it were—turned out to be a joyful occasion for family and neighbors to come together to remember a man who had touched so many lives for so many years.

Whether she knew it or not, his widow was carrying on an ancient tradition practiced by the Israelites and the surrounding cultures. On the one-year anniversary of a person's death, the surviving family and possibly the entire clan would gather around a stone table in the cemetery for a communal meal. Often, similar meals would mark future anniversaries as well, at intervals of five or ten years. Memorial meals were presumably held only for adults who had died; a meal for an infant or young child would likely have been considered inappropriate.

The early Christians, for whom communal meals were central to their worship and fellowship, undoubtedly continued this practice—to honor not only their biological family members but also their brothers and sisters in the Lord. As early as the middle of the second century, memorial meals were celebrated as a tribute to Christian martyrs.

In the context of the pagan Roman culture, these ceremonial Christian meals would often veer off into questionable territory. Some people believed the deceased actually joined the survivors for the memorial meal, and some continued the practice of praying for the dead. When the Eucharist was celebrated as a memorial meal in honor of the deceased on the anniversary of his death, some people considered the dead person

---

Then you will say in the presence of the Lord *your God: I have taken the consecrated portion out of my house; I have also given it to the Levite, the foreign resident, the fatherless, and the widow, according to all the commands You gave me. I have not violated or forgotten Your commands. I have not eaten any of it while in mourning, or removed any of it while unclean, or offered any of it for the dead. I have obeyed the* Lord *my God; I have done all You commanded me.*

—Deuteronomy 26:13–14 HCSB

to be present at the altar. (If you'd like to read a few particularly chilling accounts of funeral practices that mixed Christian and pagan rituals, do some research on the Latin word *refrigerium* and its accompanying abuses with regard to memorial meals.) Veneration of the dead, which had been practiced by the Israelites, became *worship* of the dead rather than respect for the dead. In Isaiah 65, God has some choice words for those who desecrated burial grounds with their lavish feasting, drunkenness, and secret activities: "These people continually provoke Me to My face, sacrificing in gardens, burning incense on bricks, sitting among the graves, spending nights in secret places, eating swine's flesh, and putting polluted broth in their bowls. . . . These practices are smoke in My nostrils, a fire that burns all day long" (Isa. 65:3–5 HCSB).

Memorial meals are another example of a meaningful and useful tradition that was discarded largely because of the abuses associated with it. It's sad, really. As a volunteer with a local hospice organization, I can see the value in reviving the practice of this tradition in an appropriate and culturally relevant way. (And in a *simple* way; already I'm envisioning an entrepreneur or two capitalizing on this suggestion by building an elaborate Memorial Meal Banquet Facility: "Honor your departed loved one with us! Our certified Memorial Meal Planner will handle all the details for you!") In the end, the Southern widow proved she knew how to grieve after all; the culturally relevant picnic she hosted served as a beautiful tribute to her husband.

Death practices have a transformative value.
People in both the world of the Bible and in the modern world
have used death to transform either themselves or others.

—RACHEL S. HALLOTE, *DEATH, BURIAL, AND*
AFTERLIFE IN THE BIBLICAL WORLD

Many Americans, though, are woefully unprepared to grieve. As a culture, we try to hide death, cheat death, trick death, deny death, all in a vain hope that death will just go away. We've lost the ability to grieve in a healthy and sound manner, which is why the hospice movement and an abundance of grief-related ministries have cropped up over the last thirty years or so. When we are unable to accept death and mourn effectively, we deflect our grief by projecting our anger, our sorrow, our helplessness onto others. The end result is often blame and bitterness. We think we've dealt with our loved one's passing, while all we've done is postponed the inevitable confrontation of our loss.

"Firsts" are especially difficult occasions for those left behind when a loved one dies. The first Christmas, wedding anniversary, birthday, even New Year's Eve—whatever celebration was significant to you and the one who died—those days loom before you for weeks, if not months, in advance. Early on, you begin wondering how on earth you're ever going to make it through the day.

Worst of all is the date of the person's death, a date you wish would fall right off the calendar. Imagine how differently you would approach that

---

Then he commanded them: "I am about to be gathered to my people. Bury me with my fathers in the cave in the field of Ephron the Hittite. The cave is in the field of Machpelah, near Mamre, in the land of Canaan. This is the field Abraham purchased from Ephron the Hittite as a burial site. Abraham and his wife Sarah are buried there, Isaac and his wife Rebekah are buried there, and I buried Leah there. The field and the cave in it {were purchased} from the Hittites." When Jacob had finished instructing his sons, he drew his feet into the bed and died. He was gathered to his people.

—GENESIS 49:29–33 HCSB

POTLUCK PRELUDE

On a lighter note, the Sunday ritual of going out to eat after church also has its roots in the group meals of the early church—sort of. Acts tells us that the followers of Christ met on the first day of the week to break bread and worship the Lord. First Corinthians 11 even gives us a glimpse of Christians behaving badly during those communal meals, the preludes to our modern-day potluck suppers.

Typically, the meal followed this pattern: Christians would meet in a home large enough to accommodate all of them. Everyone would bring food and drink to share. They would all sing those psalms and hymns and spiritual songs that the apostle Paul loved to write about, and then they'd go about making melody in their hearts. They would pray. They would eat. At some point, they would commemorate the Last Supper with bread and wine.

The order of those activities isn't always clear. But what is clear is that sometime during the first century, the gatherings had become so large that accommodating everyone for a meal had become unwieldy. Communion became a separate time of celebration.

Fast-forward to the contemporary church culture in the U.S., where your pastor may occasionally make a tongue-in-cheek comment about ending the service in time to beat the Baptists or the Presbyterians or the Episcopalians to the restaurants. That's all well and good, and I've usually enjoyed those after-church gatherings. But often that ritual finds friends eating with friends and relatives eating with relatives—if they're still speaking to each other after the hassle of trying to get everyone ready for church on time.

Enter the potluck, where the entire church is assembled whether you like the entire church or not, and where you're likely to take a stab at the roast beef just as the sweet-faced young thing whom you're *sure* is flirting with your husband offers to pour a glass of iced tea for you.

Oh my, these church suppers can get messy, can't they? Thank God for that.

date if you were planning a creative way to spend the day instead of wasting your precious emotional energy dreading it. While the idea of a memorial meal works well for a large family or circle of friends, you can honor the person you loved in a special way even if you're alone. You can make a point of spending a difficult anniversary doing something you and your loved one enjoyed doing together—going to a movie or a sporting event, for example, or indulging in a pint of Baskin-Robbins ice cream in the flavor *she* loved but you didn't.

And yes, the grief will surface again—on that day and on future days, whether you are alone or surrounded by a loving and supportive group of friends or family members. But you will be facing your grief rather than running from it, and that will help you accept not just your loved one's death but also the overall reality of death.

One word of caution: if it's been many years since your loved one died and you feel you have handled your grief well, it's probably best not to try to introduce this practice on behalf of that person unless you feel compelled to do so. It's likely to feel hollow and empty if a great deal of time has passed; I'm sure that would be the case for my husband and myself, who lost our parents between fifteen and thirty years ago. My brother calls me

---

Then Joseph went to bury his father, and all Pharaoh's servants, the elders of his household, and all the elders of the land of Egypt went with him, along with all Joseph's household, his brothers, and his father's household. Only their children, their sheep, and their cattle were left in the land of Goshen. Horses and chariots went up with him; it was a very impressive procession.

—GENESIS 50:7–9 HCSB

each year on the anniversary of our mother's death, and that's all the ritual I need at this point.

The ancient Israelites, as we know all too well, did not always please God. At times they drew from the rituals and traditions of the heathen cultures around them, including burial and mourning practices that were an abomination in God's eyes. It's not known whether it was the Israelites or the other Canaanites who initiated the memorial meal practice. Some believe that biblical accounts of a deceased person being "gathered to his people" not only meant that the deceased had joined those who had died earlier but also served as the basis for memorial meals, in which the surviving family "gathered" to their people as well. It is clear that it was a common enough ritual in the first century for the Jews who became followers of Christ to carry the tradition of memorial meals with them into their newfound faith.

For us as twenty-first century Christians, the practice can help bring some much-needed balance to our surrounding culture, a culture that overwhelmingly strives to deny the reality of death. More importantly, honoring the memory of the people we loved can help us grieve in a healthy way. One day, we'll be able to help someone else do the same.

Chapter 9

Spiritual Mentoring

One of the most marvelous little documents shedding light on the life of the early church is an anonymous first-century pastoral resource known as the *Didache*. Perhaps because of the rightful prominence given to the Bible, the *Didache* (pronounced DID-ah-kay or DID-ah-key, depending on whom you ask) is largely unknown among the laity. When I first learned about it, once again I felt sad to think of missed opportunities to learn from ancients who had gone before me.

In the thirty years I spent in church services and Bible studies, I can't recall anyone ever mentioning the *Didache*. Given my love of strange-sounding words, I would have remembered the word *Didache*. I think back particularly to the intense days of the 1970s Jesus People Movement when we were trying so hard to be a latter-day manifestation of the first-century church. There we were, groping in the dark, trying to figure out how best to grow in our faith and to disciple others as well, when all the time the work had been done for us by the early Christians we were trying to emulate. We just didn't know it.

Before I describe the discipleship program outlined in the *Didache*, here's my disclaimer: I believe with all my heart that when a person comes to genuine faith in Christ, there's nothing to stop that believer from being baptized and becoming a full member of the family of God. Formal training is not necessary. That said, I also believe this: We could do a whole lot worse than providing the kind of formal training the early Christians insisted that new converts undergo.

My *Didache* scholar of choice, Aaron Milavec, tells me that *didache* is a Greek word that refers to the training a master tradesman provided to an apprentice. In the context of the early church, the "master" took on the form of a mentor in walking the new believer through the early stages of his personal faith life as well as the communal life of the church. Milavec also informs me through his excellent, thousand-page book titled *The Didache* that originally the Christian manual was so widely known and used that it bore no title. Eventually, it came to be called "The Training of the Lord through the Twelve Apostles to the Gentiles." Or, as Milavec titled one section of his book, "a life-transforming training program."

The early church considered such a program—which lasted two to three years according to other documents—to be essential, and for good reasons, the main one being the persecution the new convert was almost

---

Mentoring often involves little things, such as showing someone attention and encouraging his or her walk in the Lord.

—MEL WALKER IN *MENTORING THE NEXT GENERATION*

A MODEL MENTOR

For a biblical example of the value of mentoring, look at the life of Barnabas, the "son of encouragement." It was he who urged the followers of Christ to welcome Paul—the former church persecutor known as Saul—into their fellowship and later spent a year with Paul encouraging the Gentile believers in Antioch. Just as significant was the confidence he displayed in Mark even after Mark had deserted them, which rankled Paul. But Barnabas apparently saw something in Mark that wouldn't allow him to give up on him, and his confidence paid off: some time later, Paul wrote these words: "Get Mark and bring him with you, for he is useful in my ministry" (2 Tim. 4:11 NRSV). And that's the mark of an effective spiritual mentor—bringing people to spiritual maturity so they may be useful in ministry.

certain to experience. New believers needed to know just what they were getting into, and the church wanted to prepare them for the refining fire to come. Also, since the early church held all things in common, they needed to be certain that people who said they wanted to join the community were genuinely committed to Christ and to their fellow Christians; a three-year probation period would most certainly root out any scoundrels seeking to live off the good graces of others.

Then too, it's not as if books and literacy abounded in the first century; you couldn't hand a new convert a copy of the Bible, which didn't even

A pupil is not above his teacher; but everyone,
after he has been fully trained, will be like his teacher.

—LUKE 6:40 NASB

have a New Testament yet, and a copy of the *Didache* and be done with it. Never would I have thought that I would make the following statement, but here goes: Our widespread literacy, and the gazillions of books we have at our disposal, just may have robbed us of a powerful opportunity to be trained in the faith and train others in return. The availability of books makes it all too easy for us to go it alone.

I was once the only retreatant in residence at a renewal center and as a result had three women attending to my every need, just as they would have had to do for a large group. Never mind the guilt I felt; I'm sure this saintly trio could have used a couple of days off, but leave it to me to choose those exact days to seek some solitude in their midst. One of the women assumed I was there for spiritual direction, and although I was not, I figured it was only polite for me to let her direct me, if that's what she wanted. When I entered her office, I noticed a beautiful book on her lap, something intended for use in a personal retreat. Wow! I thought. She's giving me a book! Just what I always wanted!

But no. She set the book aside. "I had planned to just give you that book to use while you're here, but I decided against it," she said, preparing me for the more personal, one-on-one mentoring that was to come. "That's too easy—just hand a person a book and that's the end of it. That's not what God has called me to do." I doubt that's what God has called any of us to do, but that's what I've done too many times, because that's the way most

---

The word mentor *is not in the Bible. But the concept is written all over the New Testament in the ministry of Jesus and of the apostles—as well as in instructions for the rest of us. . . . God has written the mentor concept into human nature, and that is why the concept is written into the Bible.*

—LYNN ANDERSON, *HEARTLIGHT MAGAZINE*

of us, including me, were "trained" as Christians. In addition to reading our Bibles, we had piles of books and lists of books, and that was the end of our formal training. Granted, many churches do offer courses for new believers, and nearly every church requires some formal instruction prior to

THREE YEARS OF TRAINING

A person wanting to be baptized had to pass muster on several levels. First, she had to be recommended by a present member of the church, who would have to attest to her genuine intention and the authenticity of her faith. Second, she had to undergo a three-year trial period, not unlike that of a novitiate entering a monastery today. The three years involved both doctrinal instruction and moral training. Finally, she underwent an examination with regard to both her knowledge and her conduct.

Only then could she enter into a specific program of preparation for baptism, for a period coinciding approximately with our current Lenten season. During that time she would receive more doctrinal and scriptural instruction, memorize the Apostles' Creed, and have exorcisms pronounced over her each day. In addition, she would be initiated into certain church practices, such as fasting and keeping a vigil. That would come in handy when she finally—finally!—was ready to be baptized, because she had to fast from Good Friday through Easter Sunday, and maintain an all-night vigil following her evening baptism on Holy Saturday. She was now allowed to receive communion.

Around the fourth century, those who were about to be baptized first faced west (the direction of sundown and darkness), proclaimed, "I renounce thee, Satan, and all thy following"—and spit forcefully. Then they turned to the east (the direction of sunrise and the risen Christ) and proclaimed, "I believe and bow before Thee and all Thy servants, O Father, Son, and Holy Spirit."

baptism, but even those are a far cry from the kind of mentoring the early church required.

Which brings me to what they required and back to my scholar, Milavec, who indicated that in one of the first steps in the program, the mentor began to prepare the convert for potential problems with family and friends. How could we in today's churches have missed that crucial first step? Some of us were shocked that others were so negative—even hostile—at what we considered the good news about the change in our lives. We didn't expect that kind of reaction, and we were left to fend for ourselves in dealing with it. Our newfound brothers and sisters simply shook their heads in dismay or railed against the heathen. Seldom were we given—or did we later give to others—any practical guidance on how to handle the opposition we faced.

Subsequent steps as outlined in the *Didache* involved disposing of personal resources in order to benefit the Christian community and learn how to live communally; teachings on the major moral and ethical demands of the faith; instruction on self-examination with regard to sin, living a life of dependence on God, and the requirements of living in community such as conflict resolution and the sharing of resources; and lessons on the importance of, and procedures associated with, rituals such as baptism and the Eucharist. The assigned mentors walked the converts through the entire three years of training, in part in order to discern their level of commitment to Christ and the community. Only with the mentor's approval could the convert be baptized and considered a full member of the church of Jesus Christ.

Imagine how different the church would be today if we had retained one simple aspect of this extensive training program: the three-year commitment of a mentor to the life of a new believer. Modify the program in any way you like, abolish the stringent requirements for baptism, or eliminate the training altogether—just retain that one element, that relationship

MILK AND HONEY

Hippolytus's *Church Order* mentions that a chalice of milk and honey was offered to new believers after they took the bread during their first communion. What a wonderful symbol! Not only was milk and honey the preferred nourishment for infants at the time, the combination obviously echoed the provision of the Promised Land.

"What does 'milk and honey' mean?" wrote a second-century Egyptian Christian named Barnabas. "A child is first fed on milk, and afterwards on honey. In the same way after we have been given life by believing in the word of promise, we shall go on to live and possess the world."

Somewhere around the fourteenth century that custom disappeared. At least it lasted that long; in only the first two centuries of the church, the chalice of milk and honey was followed by a chalice of water, symbolizing purity and baptism. Only then was the new communicant allowed to receive the wine, the blood of Christ. Each element of first communion was steeped in unmistakable spiritual symbolism for the new believer. Why did these elements of the Lord's Supper disappear? We simply don't know.

with a mentor who would say to a new believer: "Look, the going may get rough. You're experiencing joy right now, but you're likely to face opposition, hard work, and even doubts on the road ahead. But I want to assure you that I'll be right here, walking this path with you, teaching you about

Be imitators of me, as I also am of Christ.

—1 CORINTHIANS 11:1 HCSB

God and showing you how to live the way he wants you to. I will not leave you. I will be at your side for at least the next three years."

Oh, my. I wonder how different my first few years as a Christian would have been if only someone had spoken those words to me and delivered on them as well. And I wonder what the next three years will be like if I speak those words to a new convert today and deliver on them over the next thirty-six months or more. Sure, it would take time and effort, and it would complicate my life to no end. Getting all tangled up in the life of a new believer can be exhausting; I hate to think what life would have been like for my mentor had I been assigned one back in 1972. But I also can't imagine anything more valuable in laying a solid foundation for the life of a new Christian. Makes me want to go out and get somebody converted right now so I can get started with the whole mentoring thing.

Chapter 10

Spiritual Direction

Those of us who have been immersed in the evangelical world some-times have missed out on a wealth of rich spiritual experiences. I was firmly planted in that world when a friend suggested I read a series of novels by Susan Howatch about the Church of England. Well, that suggestion came close to blasphemy on three counts: first, the Anglican Church was hardly known for its evangelical leanings; second, at the time I lived and read by the motto, "Life is too short for fiction"; and third, Susan Howatch—*Susan Howatch?* She of the British historical sagas, *Cashelmara* and *Penmarric* and the like? How could anything of spiritual value come from her keyboard?

I relented and thus flirted with blasphemy, only to discover that, first, the Anglican Church indeed has its evangelical component; second, the remainder of my life was too short to read all the fiction I now wanted to read; and third, Susan Howatch—yes, Susan Howatch! She had plenty to say that was of spiritual value. And most valuable to me was her description of the practice of spiritual direction, something I confess I had never heard of before reading the books in the series.

Through her characters, Howatch demonstrated the practice of spiritual direction at its best. The various members of the clergy who populate the series would regularly seek direction from another cleric, someone who was a professional colleague but not a close friend. Howatch's handling of their sessions made it clear that the director was not acting as a detached therapist or counselor but was more of a combination caretaker and companion on a spiritual journey. The director and the one seeking direction were in a relationship with each other for the long haul. A seventeenth-century writer described spiritual directors as "God's ushers" who guide us toward the ultimate Spiritual Director. What a wonderful image! I could hardly wait to meet one.

As I worked my way through the six books in the series, the desire for spiritual direction nearly overwhelmed and depressed me at the same time. I wanted what these characters were getting from their directors, which usually meant they were discovering astonishing insights into their own nature through the careful guidance of the directors. But this, after all, was fiction, and England to boot; what were the chances I could find a spiritual director this side of the pond, if, in fact, they actually existed?

Spiritual direction is about taking time to walk with another on the spiritual path. It is about discerning the subtle movement of the Holy Spirit in the ordinariness of life.

—CAROL WHITTAKER, FRANCISCAN RENEWAL CENTER, SCOTTSDALE, ARIZONA

MENTOR OR DIRECTOR?

Though some people use the terms interchangeably, a spiritual director and a spiritual mentor serve similar but distinctly different functions. Both offer encouragement and companionship as they "come alongside" believers on their spiritual journey in unique ways.

A spiritual director, however, generally has to undergo some form of training to understand and develop skills that fall outside the domain of traditional therapy or counseling but within the domain of guidance and discernment—and to be aware of pitfalls like dependency issues. A spiritual director is invaluable to both the newcomer to the faith and the mature Christian; no one outgrows the need for spiritual direction, focused as it is on living in tune with God's will, though the intensity of that need will vary over time.

A spiritual mentor serves as an intentional model, friend, and trainer for new or returning Christians. A mentor is simply a more mature Christian than the newcomer and requires no special preparation to fulfill that role in the life of a new believer (though some ministries do provide such training). Mentors help out during those fumbling early stages of growth in relationship to Christ and are generally not equipped to provide counseling or direction; they point the way rather than offer solutions.

But speaking the truth in love, let us grow in every way into Him who is the head—Christ. From Him the whole body, fitted and knit together by every supporting ligament, promotes the growth of the body for building up itself in love by the proper working of each individual part.

—EPHESIANS 4:15–16 HCSB

Pretty good, as it turned out. On a whim, I googled "spiritual direction." (Actually, I probably used Dogpile in those pre-Google days, but saying I dogpiled "spiritual direction" just doesn't have the same ring to it.) I came up with more hits than I had anticipated and found an abundance of certified spiritual directors in Florida and the Southeast—all of them mainline liturgical. See what I mean? We evangelical Protestants were clearly missing out on a practice that I was salivating for.

I found a spiritual director of my very own, and if I had it to do over again, I would have said something like this at the start of our first session: "I've never done this before. I have no idea what to say to you to get this thing rolling, but if you've read Susan Howatch's books, you know why I'm here and what I want." That would have saved my director a whole lot of time and bewilderment, I'm sure, because I stumbled my way through that first session. But thank the good Lord for the wisdom he gives—spiritual directors are trained to cut through the you-know-what and zero in on the heart of the matter.

The heart of my matter back then isn't relevant here. What I remember from that first session was my assignment: to place myself in the story

> *Spiritual direction differs from moral guidance, psychological counseling, and the practice of confessional, preaching, or healing ministries . . . in that it directly assists individuals in developing and cultivating their personal relationship with God. We define Christian spiritual direction, then, as help given by one Christian to another which enables that person to pay attention to God's personal communication to him or her, to respond to this personally communicating God, to grow in intimacy with this God, and to live out the consequences of the relationship.*
>
> —WILLIAM A. BARRY AND WILLIAM J. CONNOLLY
> IN *THE PRACTICE OF SPIRITUAL DIRECTION*

of Jesus' baptism and see what God had to say to me through that scenario. Well, now, this was nothing like what the Brits had done in those novels—theirs were intense sessions, heavy on spiritual psychology—but I figured my director was just happy to usher me to the door and give me some busy work until our next session, when I would hopefully be a bit more focused and coherent. Frankly, I didn't expect a whole lot to come from this assignment; I mean really, how much insight did she expect me to glean from such a simple activity?

With absolutely nothing to do until our next session twenty-four hours later—I was making a silent retreat at the time—I decided to give it a shot. Today I am amazed that God even bothered with me that day. I was almost humorously arrogant, challenging the Bible to show me something I didn't already know and hadn't already seen. I went back to my sparsely furnished room at the retreat center and read the story of Jesus' baptism with all the enthusiasm of a corpse. With zero expectation I obediently settled into the rocking chair in my cell, as my director had suggested, closed my eyes, and tried to think of myself standing on the banks of the Jordan River. After too many minutes thinking ridiculous thoughts such as wondering what I would wear if I really was invited to Jesus' baptism, I eventually got serious.

Still, the exercise seemed pointless. I sat and thought and rocked and asked God if this was a royal waste of time and imagined some more and rocked some more, and then it happened. In my imagination I saw Jesus turn to the crowd on the shoreline and beckon me to come to him. Me!

If we live by the Spirit, let us also be guided by the Spirit.

—GALATIONS 5:25 NRSV

I naturally looked around to make sure he meant me, and then he called me by name. He wanted to baptize me himself.

Much more happened in that scene, but retelling a spiritual experience like that is a bit like describing a dream: the only person it means anything in the world to is you—the people you're talking to have nodded off before you get anywhere near the good part. Suffice it to say that the "simple" activity I was so reluctant to participate in proved to be among the most profound and powerful experiences of my life. In less than an hour, I was able to see one aspect of my relationship with God with greater clarity than I had in the previous thirty years combined.

My director has not given me busywork. While there's no way she could have known how that baptism scene was to unfold in my mind, she had zeroed in on a flaw in my relationship with God—but she knew I had to see it for myself. And I did see it. I certainly did.

Our subsequent sessions, which usually last an hour, haven't always involved exercises like that one. Each session is unique and will often take a turn neither of us has anticipated. But I always come away with a fresh perspective on my life and a new insight into my relationship with God.

It wasn't until several years after my first experience with spiritual direction that I realized this was hardly a new practice. Of course, throughout the Bible leaders like Moses and Paul, as well as the later desert mothers

---

We should choose our director according to the nature of our passions. If your problem is lust, do not choose for your guide a wonder-worker who has a meal and a welcome for all comers. Choose rather an ascetic who will refuse any of the consolations of food. If you are arrogant, choose someone who is harsh and unyielding, not someone who is gentle and accommodating.

—JOHN CLIMACUS, SEVENTH-CENTURY ABBOT OF SINAI

and fathers, provided spiritual direction, as have Christians through the centuries.

The specific type of spiritual direction we have today, though, more closely resembles that of a later period in history. Though the sixteenth-century mystic Ignatius of Loyola doesn't qualify as an "ancient," he wrote the book on making a retreat, *Spiritual Exercises.* In that book and in his surviving letters, he attached great significance to spiritual direction, which formed the backbone of his ministry to members of religious orders like himself. Equally important was Francis de Sales in the seventeenth century, who provided a structure for direction that also helped shape today's form of the practice.

I suspect spiritual direction is more popular and more prevalent today than ever, especially now that evangelicals are joining their more liturgical brothers and sisters in seeking out directors of their own. There are so many books on spiritual direction that I can hardly keep up with all the new releases, which I try mightily to do.

If this practice appeals to you but you'd rather take a look at spiritual direction in the context of a great story, you can't do better than Susan Howatch and her Church of England series, also known as the Starbridge series. And if, like me, you find yourself salivating, head for Google to find a solid Christian spiritual director near you who is ready to join you on your spiritual journey.

And what you have heard from me in the presence of many witnesses,
commit to faithful men who will be able to teach others also.

—2 TIMOTHY 2:2 HCSB

Chapter 11

Praying the Scriptures

One of the things I "learned" early on as a baby Christian back in the 1970s was that written prayers were lifeless. With one notable exception the Lord's Prayer, of course prayers that were memorized or written out in advance could not possibly express the thoughts of our heart at the moment we were actually praying, according to thinking among some charismatics at that time. In a word, praying written prayers was like cheating. Certain pastors I knew took great pride in the heartfelt expression of their "spontaneous" public prayer, which may have been rehearsed in front of a mirror the night before.

Meanwhile, many of my Christian brothers and sisters around the world were happily praying from a book full of written prayers, blissfully unaware that God was paying no attention to them whatsoever—or so

THE BOOK OF COMMON PRAYER

These don't qualify as praying the Scriptures, but the following prayers based on the Scriptures from the *Book of Common Prayer* should be sufficient to give you an idea of the treasure that is stored between its pages.

The first is my favorite, an evening prayer that allows me to catch my breath and hold it for one sacred moment between the rush of the day and the wishful thinking that the evening will be quieter:

> O Lord, support us all the day long, until the shadows lengthen, and the evening comes, and the busy world is hushed, and the fever of life is over, and our work is done. Then in thy mercy, grant us a safe lodging, and a holy rest, and peace at the last. Amen.

A friend directed my attention to the following prayer, which is intended for a sick person to pray in the morning. She's a woman of sound mind and body, a whole lot healthier than I am, yet she prays this prayer each morning:

> This is another day, O Lord. I know not what it will bring forth, but make me ready, Lord, for whatever it may

So shall My word be that goes forth from My mouth;
it shall not return to Me void, but it shall accomplish what I please,
and it shall prosper in the thing for which I sent it.

—ISAIAH 55:11 NKJV

be. If I am to stand up, help me to stand bravely. If I am to sit still, help me to sit quietly. If I am to lie low, help me to do it patiently. And if I am to do nothing, let me do it gallantly. Make these words more than words, and give me the Spirit of Jesus. Amen.

Finally—at least for my purpose here—there's this one, which I ought to pray every time I walk into church with an attitude, which of course I'm not saying actually happens but just in case it ever did—well, here's what I ought to pray:

> O Almighty God, who pours out on all who desire it the spirit of grace and of supplication: Deliver us, when we draw near to you, from coldness of heart and wanderings of mind, that with steadfast thoughts and kindled affections we may worship you in spirit and in truth; through Jesus Christ our Lord. Amen.

Now I ask you: who could have a problem with those prayers? Those are only three of the many in the *Book of Common Prayer,* and they're all rooted in Scriptural admonitions and truths.

By praying the scriptures out loud you are speaking God's will for your life into existence. Hearing the Word . . . causes your faith to rise. There is power in the spoken Word.

—CAROL ANN KONONOVA, AUTHOR OF *PRAYING IN VICTORY*

you'd think, given the teaching on prayer that many of us had been exposed to. I'm not exaggerating; we were taught about the kind of prayer God listened to and warned against the kind God turned a deaf ear to. Our leaders, it seemed, had the inside skinny on God's listening habits.

Well now. Their warnings presented a multitude of problems, not the least of which was the fact that the book full of written prayers that other Christians were praying was the biblical book of Psalms. Moreover, the rest of the Bible offered a wealth of words that expressed the prayerful thoughts, intentions, and petitions of their human authors. (No point in even discussing resources our pastors considered useless, such as the *Book of Common Prayer* and similar books used by liturgical churches. You'd think the folks in those churches, if they could even be considered Christians, were only marginally aware of what pleased God.)

If I seem to be dwelling a bit too much on what we had been taught way back then, here's why: the book that turned around my thinking on written prayers was written by—you guessed it—a charismatic. Of all things! Through his book *Praying the Scriptures,* Judson Cornwall (is that a great name or what?) reminded me of the deep, authentic prayer life I'd had decades earlier when I regularly prayed portions of the Bible back to God, before I realized that I was committing a charismatic gaffe.

Unlike me, the ancients had no false teachings to unlearn about how to pray to God. The Israelites, the early Christians, the desert dwellers all understood the value of the Bible as a source of prayer. As Cornwall wrote, the Bible is not only a "textbook" on prayer, useful for instruction, but also

I am ready to perform My Word.

—JEREMIAH 1:12 NKJV

Jump-Start Your Prayer Life

Here's a sampling of psalms, or portions thereof, that are great starting points for praying the Scriptures. All can be prayed word for word or with minor modifications, like substituting "you" when God is spoken of in the third person:

Psalm 2:1–6

Psalm 5

Psalm 8

Psalm 13

Psalm 25:1–7, 11, 20–21

Psalm 51

Psalm 61:1–5

Psalm 63:1–8

Psalm 71

Psalm 84

Psalm 88:1–2

Psalm 89:1–8

Psalm 104

Psalm 123

Psalm 130:1–6

Psalm 141

Psalm 144

Psalm 145

Praying the scriptures is more than just a method of praying:
It is praying God's heart and mind.

—Frank Martin, World Gospel Mission

literally a prayer book: "What seems to have been forgotten by some of today's generation"—hmm, I wonder whom he's referring to?—"is that the Bible can also become the very prayer we need to pray."

For years, I opened many of my prayers with these words of David from the New American Standard Bible, the translation I used when I began memorizing the book of Psalms in the 1970s; here's the 1995 version:

O LORD, You have searched me and known me.
You know when I sit down and when I rise up;
You understand my thought from afar.
You scrutinize my path and my lying down,
And are intimately acquainted with all my ways.
Even before there is a word on my tongue,
Behold, O LORD, You know it all. (Ps. 139:1–4)

Today, I'm sometimes more inclined toward using the paraphrase of those same verses in *The Message,* with its direct style of language:

GOD, investigate my life; get all the facts firsthand.
I'm an open book to you;
even from a distance, you know what I'm thinking.
You know when I leave and when I get back;
I'm never out of your sight.
You know everything I'm going to say
before I start the first sentence.

If you abide in Me, and My words abide in you, you will ask what you desire, and it shall be done for you.

—JOHN 15:7 NKJV

Those verses have always seemed to be a fitting way to begin praying, with their reminder that God knows everything I'm about to say. No need to inform God of the facts; I can go straight into pouring out my heart and seeking the wisdom I need.

The book of Psalms is a great place to find appropriate verses when you start the practice of praying the Scriptures, but it's hardly the only place. Look at these prayers, just a few of the many in the Bible; any one of us could pray these words from *The Message* with sincerity, depending on the circumstances:

Speak, GOD. I'm your servant, ready to listen.

—1 SAMUEL 3:9

The tears stream from my eyes,
an artesian well of tears,
Until you, GOD, look down from on high,
look and see my tears.
When I see what's happened to the young women in the city,
the pain breaks my heart.

—LAMENTATIONS 3:49–51

Give your servants fearless confidence in preaching your Message,
as you stretch out your hand to us in healings and miracles and
wonders done in the name of your holy servant Jesus.

—ACTS 4:29–30

GOD, pick up the pieces.
Put me back together again.
You are my praise!

—JEREMIAH 17:14

"Yes! Come, Master Jesus!"

—REVELATION 22:20

The Bible also provides numerous mentions of prayers, though the exact words are not given. Let's face it; we've all experienced those times when we have not known how to pray for someone else. The Scriptures offer us endless inspiration for fresh ways to petition God on behalf of others as evidenced in these verses, also taken from *The Message*:

We pray for you all the time—pray that our God will make you fit for what he's called you to be, pray that he'll fill your good ideas and acts of faith with his own energy so that it all amounts to something.

—2 THESSALONIANS 1:11

So this is my prayer: that your love will flourish and that you will not only love much but well.

—PHILIPPIANS 1:9

I couldn't stop thanking God for you—every time I prayed, I'd think of you and give thanks. But I do more than thank. I ask—ask the God of our Master, Jesus Christ, the God of glory—to make you intelligent and discerning in knowing him personally, your eyes focused and clear, so that you can see exactly what it is he is calling you to do, grasp the immensity of this glorious way of life he has for Christians.

—EPHESIANS 1:16–18

There's a third way to pray the Scriptures, and this is the one evangelicals are probably most familiar with. Unfortunately, this method resulted in fairly widespread abuse among some segments of the church,

Heaven and earth will pass away, but My words will not pass away.

—MARK 13:31 NASB

particularly among charismatics, over the last thirty years. It involves praying God's own words back to him, as in this example based on John 14:14: "Lord, you said that if we ask anything in your name, you will do it. I'm asking you now to . . ." The potential for abuse is apparent; too many leaders advised their flocks that if they asked God to give them a Cadillac, or widescreen TV, or a million dollars, he would do it for them—no, he *had* to do it for them!

So let's try another example. This one is based on Philippians 4:6–7: "Lord, your Word tells us to be anxious for nothing but to bring our requests to you in a spirit of thanksgiving. As I bring you my anxieties, I ask that you would give me your peace." No matter what your prayer concern is, you're likely to find verses in the Bible that you can pray back to God in this way.

Some of this commentary may seem like Prayer 101, but we're all at different points on our journey of faith. New believers may be hearing about praying the Scriptures for the first time, and veteran believers may not yet have experienced the freedom of praying the Scriptures or written prayers of any kind. Our ancestors in the faith would find that to be puzzling; to them, there was no richer source of words to pray—especially when their own words would just not come.

Chapter 12

Fixed-Hour Prayer

Ideliberated way too long over how to title this chapter. Should it be "The Daily Offices"? To contemporary ears, that sounds like a news bureau. How about "The Divine Hours"? Accurate, but perhaps too monastic and medieval. One thing I knew: it couldn't be *opus dei*, Latin for "work of the Lord." No, Dan Brown and his heretical *The Da Vinci Code* pretty much guaranteed that that particular phrase would be linked with an allegedly sinister religious organization, at least for the foreseeable future. Later I settled on "The Work of the Lord," but fixed-hour prayer has very little to do with what we think of as work.

So here we are with "Fixed-Hour Prayer," which has everything to do with following a regular, daily schedule of rigorous prayer, much as religious communities of all faiths have done for centuries. The Christian tradition stems from the Jewish practice of praying three times a day. Let me assure you that this practice is not only relevant to lovers of God in the third millennium but also achievable by the overworked, the over-committed, and the over-obligated among us.

I know it's achievable because I know people who achieve it, most notably Phyllis Tickle, the author of the multi-volume *The Divine Hours* series (Doubleday, 2000–2004) and a very busy woman who has followed a regular schedule of daily prayer for decades. More than once I've come upon Phyllis from behind on a crowded trade-show floor to discover that she was deep in prayer in the midst of bookselling commotion.

Phyllis will be the first to tell you of the benefits of fixed-hour prayer, but she'll also be the first to encourage you to do what you can, when you can. Her commitment to keeping the offices, as the various daily prayer times are called, has developed over many years; anyone expecting to follow a full regimen of fixed-hour prayer is bound to meet with failure and will likely give up completely.

The first thing you need to know about fixed-hour prayer, and the one thing that may cause you to exhale an enormous sigh of relief, is that the hours of prayer aren't all that fixed outside of monastic communities. There the hours are rigid; heaven help the poor monk who fails to be in his

We live in a time when the call to practice {fixed-hour} prayer clearly seems to be drawing more and more Christians to its practice. It is an ancient call, with its roots in the Jewish faith, and in the early Christian communities, and the desert where our fathers and mothers kept the tradition alive. It is a call that seems to be crying out for some new ways to think about this prayerful discipline.

—ROBERT BENSON IN *VENITE: A BOOK OF DAILY PRAYER*

assigned spot at the final sounding of the bell signaling the start of that particular office. One thing a monastery visitor learns right away about monks is that they don't try to hide their displeasure with their brothers just because visitors are present.

Let me describe the offices first and then suggest how you can adapt and simplify them for a nonmonastic lifestyle.

The monastic schedule requires that the community come together for prayer at the following times (the Latin names by which these offices are known appear in parentheses): in the early morning (*lauds,* usually at 3 a.m.); at 6 a.m. (*prime*); at 9 a.m. (*terce,* referred to as the "third hour" in the New Testament); at noon (*sext,* the sixth hour); at 3 p.m. (*none,* the ninth hour); at 6 p.m. (*vespers*); before bedtime (*compline,* anywhere from sundown to 9 p.m.); and *vigil* (midnight). The offices include Scripture reading, written prayers, psalms, the Lord's Prayer, and possibly a hymn or two.

Other than lauds, compline, and vigil, the hours coincide with the hours when the forum bells would ring in cities throughout the Roman Empire, marking certain activities in the business day. Jews who were dispersed throughout the empire longed for the sense of community they had lost, so they would stop and pray at the sound of the bells, knowing their prayers were joined with those of other Jews at the same hour. The early Christians continued the tradition they had followed as Jews.

If you ever have a chance to visit a monastery, take advantage of it. There's nothing that quite compares with the jolt you get when you see a monk running across a courtyard, his black skirts flying, in a desperate

---

They are also to stand every morning to give thanks and praise to the
LORD, and likewise in the evening.

—1 CHRONICLES 23:30 HCSB

attempt to be in place in the choir when the office begins—and then to see the peace and serenity that envelops him and relaxes his entire demeanor once he joins his voice with that of his brothers. The offices have a settling effect on both the monks and the visitors; they anchor the day and ground you to an experience that is at once ancient and relevant.

So how does this practice fit in to a nine-to-five—or rather, 24/7—twenty-first century lifestyle? If you're supposed to be working at your desk or punching a time card at 9:00 a.m., how on earth can you also read Scripture, sing a psalm or two, pray several prescribed prayers, and sing a hymn at the same time? Ah, that's the beauty of unfixed fixed-hour prayer—a term that sounds oxymoronic but isn't. The idea is to adapt the offices so you can do what you can when you can; the purpose is to get in the habit of stopping to remember God at various intervals throughout the day. The idea is not to get hung up on doing it right, and the purpose is not to tie you down to a legalistic schedule.

First off, you may be pleased to know that only four offices are observed outside a monastic environment—morning, noon, vespers, and compline. You may also be pleased to discover how flexible the hours are: between 6 and 9 a.m. for morning prayer; between 11 a.m. and 2 p.m. for noon prayer; between 5 and 8 p.m. for vespers or evening prayer; and for compline—well, you're on your own. You observe compline right before you go to bed. My personal preference is to observe compline in a candlelit room; ending the day in this way dramatically alters what's on my mind right before I fall asleep.

Prayer should be the key of the day and the lock of the night.

—Thomas Fuller

Secondly, contemporary fixed-hour prayer books like Phyllis's have simplified and reduced the amount of text to be used at each office. Her books eliminate the vespers office as well as some of the repetition that works well in a chanted monastic service but not so well in private use. I've followed her book and found that it usually takes less than ten minutes to complete an entire office, and that's reading it at a meditative pace.

You may also be pleased to find that you no longer need an assortment of ribbons to keep your place, nor do you have to keep turning pages to find it. Everything is printed in order and in one section for each day, meaning you'll have time to say your noon prayers and eat lunch. For those who don't know what I'm talking about or why saving time to eat is such a big deal, be thankful that you don't.

Finally, you need to remember that your prayers are precious to God no matter when you pray them. Fixed-hour prayer orders your day and provides structure and spiritual discipline as well as a regular reminder about what's really important. It doesn't mean any more to God than whatever your prayer routine, or lack of routine, was in the past. To approach fixed-hour prayer rigidly and legalistically is to miss its beauty.

And here is its beauty: Not only are you prompted to turn your heart and your mind toward God at fixed intervals, you are also united in prayer with countless Christians in your time zone who are following the same routine. This realization was deeply meaningful and profound to me when I first began to keep the offices. How could I have missed that? How could I not have realized that Christians singing at noon in South Carolina

> *Seven times each day I stop and shout praises for the way*
> *you keep everything running right.*
>
> —PSALM 119:164 MSG

were doing the very same thing at the very same time as Christians in Pennsylvania and Florida, Quebec and Brazil? Or that I could join in? I was astonished!

What's more, those of us who keep the offices in the eastern time zone have the privilege of handing them off to those who keep the offices in the central time zone, contributing to what Phyllis calls a "cascade of prayer," a continuous movement of fixed-hour prayer that encircles the globe. That's a concept that takes my breath away each time I stop and consider what it means.

One more point: Nothing quite takes the place of reading the offices out loud, but given the lack of privacy in most of our lives, we'll have to settle for silent reading most of the time. Still, it's a good idea to read the offices aloud, as well as chant the psalms out loud (see page 90), whenever possible.

If you want to test the waters of fixed-hour prayer, you might want to start by incorporating one office into your life on a daily basis. My vote would go to compline, but if you feel a greater need to get up at 3:00 a.m. for lauds, have at it. You may find that adding just one office a week is enough for now. And if fixed-hour prayer doesn't work for you, you'll find that out quickly enough. But if it does, never forget that you're not alone in this; you've joined a worldwide communion of Christians who are all participating in that continuous cascade of prayer.

Endeavor seven times a day to withdraw
from business and company and lift up
thy soul to God in private retirement.

—ADONIRAM JUDSON

CHANTING THE PSALMS

Chanting the psalms is a practice that's as old as the psalms themselves. I'm hardly a trained cantor, but I can assure you of this: you can make your own chanting style as simple or as complex as you want it to be. I vote for simple, but like I said, I'm no trained cantor.

Here is the best way to learn a simple method of chanting: you go to a monastery and hear for yourself how it's done. Ah, but you want to start now. Okay, let me be your untrained guide to the basics of this ancient practice.

The simplest method is to find a note that feels comfortable to you and that you feel you can sustain throughout the entire psalm (seldom do prayer books include more than a few verses of a psalm in each office, so we're talking a short amount of time). When I say "find a note," I just mean make a sound; you don't have to read music or know anything about it to do this. I speak from experience here.

Begin by chanting the first line of the psalm. In most, if not all, prayer books, you'll see an asterisk somewhere in that first line, often at the end. On the last accented syllable in the word right before the asterisk, raise your voice one note and then resume chanting on the original note. At the end of the next line—the end of the verse—drop your voice one note on the last accented syllable. If the last accented syllable in either line is a personal pronoun, maintain the original note as you chant the pronoun and raise or lower your voice one note on the accented syllable nearest the pronoun.

Well. That's as clear as the latest tax-return preparation guide, right?

About noon the next day, as they were on their journey and approaching the city, Peter went up on the roof to pray.

—ACTS 10:9 NRSV

Here's an example from Psalm 23:2, from the *Book of Common Prayer*:

He makes me lie down in green pastures
And leads me beside still waters.

Chant the first line on a single note, raising your voice one note on the "pas" syllable in "pastures." Return to the original note, lower your voice one note on the "wa" syllable in "waters," and finish on the original note. (The asterisk, by the way, marks the point at which you should pause, whether you are reading aloud or chanting the psalm.)

Now that you know how, you'd probably like to know why. Why bother chanting the psalms when you can just read them? Well, you can do either or both, of course, just at different times. I like to chant the psalms during fixed-hour prayer, but I also like to read them and meditate on them at other times. Chanting can bring the mind and body into the experience in a way different than reading aloud does, for it requires deeper concentration and a wider vocal range. But both methods are beneficial in that they incorporate the body, mind, and spirit.

As far as the pacing goes, the best way to learn about that is to go to a monastery and hear for yourself how it's done. In lieu of that, just slow down when you chant, but not in an exaggerated way. Chanting should be a comfortable spiritual experience; find the vocal range and pace that work best for you.

Once you get the hang of it, you may find that you enjoy chanting so much that you'll want to try your hand at chanting the Scripture readings or the prayers. Since they're not poems as the psalms are, you don't have to be concerned about raising or lowering a note at certain times.

When the clock strikes, it is a good time to say a prayer.
—JEREMY TAYLOR

Chapter 13

Gossiping the Gospel

G ossiping the gospel—what a great way to describe evangelism!
I borrowed that phrase from Michael Green's insightful *Evangelism in the Early Church,* in which he explores both the first Christians' attitudes toward spreading the gospel and the methods they used. As I read his text I was struck by how appropriate those attitudes and methods are for those of us who want to infect our postmodern world with the good news of Jesus Christ.

To this day, I blanch at the memory of my first stab at unnatural evangelism—a term I use to describe any form of evangelism that is not prompted by the Holy Spirit and therefore does not come from the heart. I was a new, and therefore highly impressionable, Christian, and the church I was attending had implemented a program designed to train the young adults in the fine art of door-to-door evangelism. The thought of going door to door and trying to convince people that they should fall right down on their knees and ask Jesus into their hearts didn't exactly excite me. But I obediently went to my assigned neighborhood at the appointed time, a Saturday morning. I prayed all the way there—not that people would be saved but that nobody would be home.

Unfortunately for them, way too many people were home. Those who weren't bored or offended by my shoddy and uninformed presentation of the gospel message were clearly amused by my naïveté. It probably goes without saying that no one responded with a significant degree of enthusiasm. In fact, no one responded at all, as I recall, unless you count all the rolled eyes, grunts, and chuckles.

So who came up with this idea for door-to-door evangelism anyway? I'm not sure who was the first, but I've heard many people point to the story of Ananias in the book of Acts as justification for this approach, an approach that proved highly ineffective in my own life. This was not the Ananias of Jerusalem, by the way, the one who was struck dead for lying to the apostles. This was Ananias of Damascus, who had the unfortunate experience of being singled out by God to visit the home of a man named Judas, whose house guest was none other than the notorious Saul—the same Saul who was known far and wide for persecuting Christians.

Ananias wanted nothing to do with Saul, and his response was pretty close to what mine would have been: "Master, you can't be serious" (Acts 9:13 MSG). As a matter of fact, that sounds a lot like my thoughts on that

It is the duty of every Christian to be Christ to his neighbor.

—MARTIN LUTHER

dreaded Saturday morning circa 1973. Ananias continued his objection by informing the Lord, "Everybody's talking about this man and the terrible things he's been doing, his reign of terror against your people in Jerusalem! And now he's shown up here with papers from the Chief Priest that give him license to do the same to us" (v. 14). The Lord already knew that, but he didn't let Ananias off the hook.

What Ananias didn't know was that Saul had already encountered the living Christ on the way to Damascus and that God had prepared him for this visit. That fact alone can be, and has been, used as a fairly strong argument in favor of door-to-door evangelism; we never know what's going on in a person's life or how God may have been preparing his heart for our visit. But remember this: Ananias was compelled to visit Saul through a personal and dramatic vision of the Lord.

While dramatic accounts like this one and the encounter between Philip and the Ethiopian eunuch (see Acts 8:26–40) are riveting enough, a more common means of gossiping the gospel in the first few centuries involved simple hospitality—and not always on the part of the Christian. Priscilla and Aquila opened their home to Paul, their colleague in tent-making; it's not clear whether they were Christians when he moved in, but they certainly were when he moved out. They went right along with him to Ephesus, where they were able to further instruct Apollos in the gospel. Apollos in turn became an effective evangelist to the Jews.

At some point, Priscilla and Aquila opened their home to the entire Christian community. Paul writes, "Say hello to Priscilla and Aquila, who

---

Then He said to them, "Go into all the world
and preach the gospel to the whole creation."

—MARK 16:15 HCSB

have worked hand in hand with me in serving Jesus. They once put their lives on the line for me. And I'm not the only one grateful to them. All the non–Jewish gatherings of believers also owe them plenty, to say nothing of the church that meets in their house" (Rom. 16:3–5 MSG).

By the way, though much of what passes for Christian home décor today might be looked upon as tacky, adding decorative Christian items to the home is hardly a recent phenomenon. I once read where archeologists discovered lamps dating to New Testament times that had been etched with symbols like the *ichthus,* the fish which became a Christian symbol. Numerous mosaics depicting the bread and the wine have been unearthed in homes dating to that period, as have paintings of Christian symbols.

The meaning behind these decorative objects would have been apparent to other believers but lost to outsiders. If the piece was particularly striking, a non-Christian visitor to the home would likely ask about it—and the piece would then become an evangelistic tool as the homeowner elaborated on its symbolism. Maybe the early Christian artisans were wary of the threat of persecution, or maybe they just understood the value of using a symbol to open evangelistic doors, but whatever the case, we could use some of their subtlety today.

Outside the home, the spread of Christianity was very much a Starbucks-type phenomenon. By the time Christianity came along, the major cities of the Roman Empire had long been established as centers for philosophical debate. Ideas great and small were routinely and enthusiastically discussed in the first-century equivalent of coffee houses and bars and

---

Evangelism as the New Testament describes it is not child's play.
Evangelism is work, often hard work. Yet it is not drudgery.
It puts a person in good humor, and makes him truly human.

—OSWALD C. HOFFMAN

parks—any place where men were free to meet and relax and talk for hours on end.

This atmosphere was ideal for someone like Paul, who seemed to love to talk about Jesus and how he could be nothing less than the Son of God. I think I would have liked Paul, despite his apparent abrasiveness; in any event, I would have been right there in the marketplace discussing the deeper issues of life with anyone who cared to join me, lingering for hours over whatever the beverage of the day would have been.

In addition to talking about Jesus in public places where spiritual discussion could flourish, the earliest Christians had a ready-made venue for evangelistic preaching: the local synagogue. Paul in particular took advantage of the synagogues' openness to appeal to the Jewish faithful by showing *through the Scriptures* how Jesus fulfilled the promises of the long-awaited Messiah. As the gospel spread to the Gentiles—and as the synagogues closed their doors and pulpits to Jesus followers around the turn of the first century—Christians turned more toward open-air evangelism in secular venues, as modeled by Paul at the Areopagus.

And what a model that is! Paul laid the groundwork by engaging some of the Athenian intellectuals in private conversation. In time, they asked him to speak about his ideas publicly. Paul was clearly in his element; the public square in Athens known as the Areopagus, or Mars Hill, attracted both locals and visitors from around the world who hung around

---

But I count my life of no value to myself,
so that I may finish my course and
the ministry I received from the Lord Jesus,
to testify to the gospel of God's grace.

—ACTS 20:24 HCSB

Spoiling the Egyptians

This is another great phrase, one that came to be used in the second century to describe the way Christians used points of intersection between secular thought and Christ's teachings to their evangelistic advantage, much the way Paul did on the Areopagus. After all, the early church reasoned, we teach that God created everything and everyone; how can we not expect to find some areas of agreement between Judeo-Christian beliefs and pagan or secular thought?

The first Christians apparently relished the idea of underscoring the truth of the gospel by using the words of the non-Christian writers and thinkers that the society greatly revered and showing how Jesus' teachings supported the very thoughts they expressed. The early Christians were likewise unafraid to borrow the language and ideas of pagan religions whenever pagan thought happened to coincide with Christian belief. We've come full circle today, with some church leaders suggesting that our best hope of reaching an increasingly diverse, multicultural, and non-Christian society—similar to the Roman Empire—is to learn the language of society's subgroups and translate the gospel into terms relevant to those groups. And as we know from personal experience, once people get a taste of the gospel in all its truth and glory and power, they are forever spoiled from settling for anything less.

Our business is to present the Christian faith clothed in modern terms, not to propagate modern thought clothed in Christian terms. Confusion here is fatal.

—J. I. Packer

CHURCH IS FOR THE CHURCH

For the first hundred and fifty or so years of the church, believers met in private homes. The services they held were apparently designed for those who had already professed faith in Christ. After all, praising God and partaking of the Lord's Supper formed the core of their time together; how could someone who had no personal experience of faith be expected to participate with any integrity in those activities? Their teaching was limited to "preaching to the choir," its purpose being to expound on the Scriptures and teach those who already believed. Evangelism was not a function of the church service.

Can people come to know Christ in church? Absolutely! But church is not usually where evangelism should begin, and the early Christians knew that well enough. Evangelism begins when people see our transformed lives—lives that we no longer see as our own but as belonging to Christ to do as he will with them. And as we know, that always means sacrificing our own lives for other people.

"waiting for the latest tidbit on most anything," as one Bible paraphrase describes it in Acts 17:21. Little did they know what "tidbit" Paul was about to lay on them.

This is where I think we all should pause and give thanks to God for Luke, who recorded the verses that follow for posterity. I love what happens next. It's so good that I can't resist quoting Paul's first words to the crowd that had assembled: "It is plain to see that you Athenians take your

And how can they preach unless they are sent?
As it is written: How welcome are the feet of those
who announce the gospel of good things!

—ROMANS 10:15 HCSB

religion seriously. When I arrived here the other day, I was fascinated with all the shrines I came across. And then I found one inscribed To THE GOD NOBODY KNOWS. I'm here to introduce you to this God so you can worship intelligently, know who you're dealing with" (MSG).

And then he tells them who they're dealing with.

Look at how he got their attention! Not by degrading their culture, not by denouncing their religion, not by telling them how angry he was—and he was angry!—at the site of all those shrines. Nor did he hammer away at the evidence of sin throughout the land. No. Paul appealed to their religious sensibilities, no matter how skewed he considered those sensibilities to be. Paul was an immensely wise and intelligent man.

Michael Green makes this astute observation contrasting today's evangelism methods with those of the early Christians: "Much evangelism today is brash and unthinking; the intellectuals do not engage in it. This is our double loss: the practitioners do not know any theology and the theologians do not do any evangelism." He goes on to show "how flexible the early evangelists were, getting inside the mindset of pagans and Jews alike, and transposing the gospel into the appropriate key in order to intrigue and engage them. . . . They did not accommodate the gospel to the culture of the day. They did, however, move the good news out of its original Jewish dress and put Gentile clothes on it without compromising its content. Modern Christians have much to learn from their ingenuity, their fidelity, and their enculturation."

I have but one candle of life to burn, and I would rather burn it out in a land filled with darkness than in a land flooded with light.

—JOHN KEITH FALCONER

Amen to that. If you think we're living in a world in which it is difficult to communicate the gospel, imagine what it was like for the early Christians. Between the Jews who considered them to be blasphemers of the one true God and the pagans who expected them to bow down to Caesar, they didn't stand a chance—unless the Holy Spirit empowered them to withstand the opposition and transformed them to be witnesses by the sheer evidence of their character.

And that is perhaps the greatest lesson we can learn from the early evangelists. Our strategies, our methods, our programs will prove to be ineffective to the postmodern world around us without the two-pronged effect of the power and inspiration of the Holy Spirit and the everyday silent witness of our transformed lives. "The quality of their lives was blazingly distinct. . . . You could mow these Christians down, you could throw them to the lions, but you could not make them deny their Lord or hate their persecutors," Green writes.

May I quote Green one last time? "The Western Church has grown too dependent on words, and not nearly dependent enough on the power of the Holy Spirit. . . . Instead of being a community demonstrating the Lord's power, we have become one which talks incessantly."

Oh yes.

> For Christ did not send me to baptize, but to preach
> the gospel—not with clever words, so that
> the cross of Christ will not be emptied {of its effect}.
>
> —1 CORINTHIANS 1:17 HCSB

Chapter 14

Praying with Poetry

The thought of reading poetry can be a daunting one. I avoided reading verse for years because so many older poems no longer spoke while contemporary poetry, being so focused on angst, left me cold. Plus, there's the snobbery effect, the automatic branding of anyone who reads poetry as a snooty intellectual wannabe. I didn't want to be branded a wannabe of any stripe, snooty or intellectual or otherwise.

Ignorance and preconceived notions can rob us of so much pleasure, can't they? I have no clue where I got the idea that contemporary poetry was either dark and angsty and abstract beyond all understanding, or mindless and sugary and greeting-card shallow. Maybe it's because I hadn't encountered any contemporary poetry that reflected my faith. There is a wealth of exceptional poetry written by Christians and much of it is worth incorporating into our

POETS TO PRAY BY

Here's a by-no-means-comprehensive list of some poets whose works lend themselves well as prayers to God—or express a prayerful intent toward God.

Wendell Berry: A contemporary poet and farmer whose works have received several prestigious awards.

Catherine of Siena: A fourteenth-century theologian and writer who began having visions at the age of six.

Meister Eckhart: A member of the Dominican order and professor at the University of Paris. The works of this poet, who died in 1329, are becoming increasingly popular.

Francis of Assisi: We all know the "Prayer of St. Francis" ("Lord, make me an instrument of thy peace"), but Francis also wrote a number of other poems before his death in 1226.

Hadewijch of Brabant: Little is known about the life of this well-educated thirteenth-century Flemish woman, who wrote several dozen poems that we know of.

George Herbert: Religious poet known for his exquisite use of imagery, Herbert served as vicar of a rural Anglican church for several years before his death in 1633.

Hildegard of Bingen: Twelfth-century visionary.

Karol Jozef Wojtyla: This man from Poland who later became Pope John II was an accomplished poet.

My heart overflows with a beautiful thought!
I will recite a lovely poem to the king,
for my tongue is like the pen of a skillful poet.

—PSALM 45:1 NLT

Julian of Norwich: Born in 1342, Julian (or Juliana) lived in a sealed room in a church, with only two windows—one to the inside of the church and one to the outside to receive food and visitors.

Mary Oliver: The nature-oriented work of this contemporary poet is not overtly Christian verse but often directs my thoughts toward God.

Christina Rossetti: I love this poet's name and wish it were my own. I also love her beautiful lyric verse.

Mother Teresa: You know all about her, but you may not know her poetry. It's beautiful.

St. John of the Cross: Sixteenth-century poet who really did write poems other than "Dark Night of the Soul." Honest.

Teresa of Avila: A fourteenth-century religious poet with a sense of humor! (I'm especially partial to "Laughter Came from Every Brick.")

Teresa of Lisieux: Known for her childlike trust in God, the "Little Flower of Jesus" died in 1897 at the age of 24.

Also, check out these books:

Poetry as Prayer series from Pauline Books & Media, with individual titles featuring Gerard Manley Hopkins, Jessica Powers, Francis Thompson, Emily Dickinson, Francis of Assisi, Thomas Merton, Denise Levertov, and the psalms.

Praying Through Poetry: Hope for Violent Times and *Praying the Gospels Through Poetry: Lent to Easter,* both by Peggy Rosenthal (St. Anthony Messenger Press).

We all write poems. It is simply that poets are the ones who write in words.

—JOHN FOWLES

prayer life. When I discovered the poetry of contemporary writers like Pulitzer Prize-winning poet Mary Oliver, Jessica Powers, and Wendell Berry, I became a convert to contemporary poetry and a poem pray-er all at once.

But first, back to the ancients. The most obvious poet in our Judeo-Christian tradition was David, who composed his lyrical prayers to God, and all those other nameless or lesser-known psalmists whose works also appear in the book of Psalms. Hezekiah was also something of a poet; one of his poems survives in Isaiah 38:9–20. The prophet Balaam recites no fewer than seven poems in Numbers 23 and 24. New Testament examples are the Beatitudes, 1 Corinthians 13, and Colossians 2:11.

Throughout history, poets—who are contemplatives in one way or another—have expressed their relationship with God through their poetry, either directly in the form of a prayer poem or indirectly as spiritual verse. Both can be adapted for use in personal prayer. Since prayer poems are addressed directly to God, we can simply pray the words aloud, meditatively and reflectively. Either form can be used as a springboard for a prayer expressed in our own words. Often a single line or section expresses the cry of our heart, and we can find ourselves praying that one excerpt back to God.

The verses that follow come from the pen of Symeon the New Theologian, who lived in the eleventh century. His prayer poem "By What Boundless Mercy, O Savior" begins like this:

And I'll be the poet who sings your glory—
and live what I sing every day.

—Psalm 61:8 MSG

By what boundless mercy, my Savior,

have you allowed me to become a member of your body?

Me, the unclean, the defiled, the prodigal.

How is it that you have clothed me

in the brilliant garment,

radiant with the splendor of immortality,

that turns all my members into light?

As you can probably tell, Symeon was most assuredly a mystic. He tried to integrate his mystical experiences into his public life as a senator—what was he thinking?—but gave up and joined a monastery, which certainly made more sense. He later became an abbot but ran afoul of ecclesiastical authorities and was exiled to a hermitage when he was sixty years old. That's when he began writing his best-known work, a collection of poems called *Hymns of Divine Love* from which the poem above is taken.

Even if some of the language in a poem like this may not express your own heart, just reading it can offer a different perspective on your membership in the body of Christ. And most of us can easily pray that first question as one of the more profound questions of our life with God, while the following lines that end the poem serve as a reminder of what we truly are, regardless of what we think we are:

I see the beauty of it all, I can gaze on the radiance.

I have become a reflection of the light of your grace.

Poetry should be great and unobtrusive, a thing which enters into one's soul, and does not startle it or amaze it with itself, but with its subject.

—JOHN KEATS

Here's another prayer poem, this one from Ignatius of Loyola, founder of the Society of Jesus (Jesuits):

Just Because You Are My God

Just because you are my God
Oh, my God, I want to love you.
Not that I might gain eternal heaven
Nor escape eternal hell
But, Lord, to love you just because you are my God.
And not to count the cost,
To fight for you
And not to mind the wounds,
To labor and to ask for no reward
Except the knowledge
That I serve my God.

And all God's evangelicals said, "Amen."

Then there's Mechthild of Magdeburg, whose name is quite the mouthful. This thirteenth-century Christian is gaining popularity among today's evangelicals. Here are two of her poems:

I Cannot Dance

I cannot dance, Lord, unless you lead me.
If you want me to leap with abandon,

For in Him we live and move and exist, as even some of your own poets have said, "For we are also His offspring."

—ACTS 17:28 HCSB

You must intone the song.

Then I shall leap into love,

From love into knowledge,

From knowledge into enjoyment,

And from enjoyment beyond all human sensations.

There I want to remain, yet want also to circle higher still.

How the Soul Speaks to God

Lord, you are my lover,

My longing,

My flowing stream,

My sun,

And I am your reflection.

Because most poetry by its very nature is meant to be read slowly and reflectively, many poems naturally lend themselves to a prayerful approach. Even if a poem cannot be prayed directly to God, which is the case with the work of poets like Wendell Berry and Mary Oliver, it may still express an otherwise inexpressible thought of your heart. Reading an appropriate poem prayerfully can transform it into a prayer.

As a former English teacher, I hereby give you permission to erase all your negative memories of reading poetry in school and start reading it all over again—but this time with a purpose far more valuable than earning a passing grade.

Poetry is an echo, asking a shadow to dance.

—CARL SANDBURG

Chapter 15

Sacred Reading

Like most Scripture-loving evangelicals, I couldn't get enough of the Bible when I first came to faith in Christ. It never ceased to astonish me, even though I had read it as a sacred text when I was a child and had studied it as literature when I was in college. For years I followed one of those daily Bible reading plans that start you out with Genesis and Matthew in January, but after a while I realized that each year I began dreading February and March, thanks to Leviticus, Numbers, and Deuteronomy. At least I had the Psalms to help me keep my sanity; I read through the entire book of Psalms every month (five psalms every day) as well as the book of Proverbs (one chapter per day, corresponding to the day of the month). When the shine began to wear off, I switched to another Bible translation.

I was a Bible-reading fanatic.

But my obsessive attachment to the Bible didn't stop there. I also studied the Bible apart from the rigid reading schedule I kept. I spent many an evening poring over the Bible on my lap with a concordance to my left, a Bible handbook to my right, and assorted other Bible reference books scattered across the floor. You may be wondering how I had time to do anything else. I often wonder the same thing. Somehow, I managed to keep a job and go to church and have time for my friends.

And yet, with all of that reading, all of that studying, all of that memorizing (see chapter 16), none of the time I spent in the Bible qualified as the spiritual discipline known as sacred reading.

I can no longer remember who introduced me to this practice, but I will never forget my reaction. I was horrified! This person suggested I take a break from all this voracious reading and linger over smaller segments of the Word of God. He or she even had the audacity to suggest that those smaller segments could be as short as one verse, but I was to spend time, real time, precious time reading the verse over and over again, allowing God to speak to me through it.

How on earth was I supposed to read through the Bible in a year at that pace? I thought my friend was nuts. That sounded like something only a hermit would have time to do because all he had to do all day was read the Bible and pray, right? I had to work during the day and catch up on my Bible reading at night! If I didn't do that, all those recluses would be way ahead of me!

In your reading, let not your end be to seek and find out subtleties,
but to find and meet with Christ.

—THOMAS TAYLOR

GROUP *LECTIO* . . . OR MAYBE NOT

I never gave a whole lot of thought to the practice of *lectio* in a group, mainly because I've never experienced it. It wasn't until I read Thomas Keating's comments on group lectio that I realized there's a difference of opinion among lectio devotees as to whether group lectio is lectio at all.

Group lectio starts when one person reads a scriptural passage aloud four times, with a few minutes of silence after each reading. (By "group," I mean two or more people; a married couple, for instance, may benefit greatly from this kind of shared spiritual discipline.) Each participant listens to God to determine which word, phrase, or sentence he or she is to dwell on, and then proceeds with lectio as described.

The main difference—and this is where Keating seems to have a problem with using the word lectio—is that the entire group is working from one common passage of Scripture, which eliminates the highly personal step of reading a portion of the Bible that you specifically feel led to read. For that reason, Keating prefers to call the group practice "Liturgy of Lectio Divina."

M. Basil Pennington, another leader in the lectio movement and author of *Lectio Divina: Renewing the Ancient Practice of Praying the*

The years I spent wandering in the wilderness of my own ignorance and narrow thinking are more than I care to remember. I wandered for several decades when it comes to this spiritual discipline, which I found

*It is better to read a little and ponder a lot
than to read a lot and ponder a little.*

—DENIS PARSONS BURKITT

Scriptures, suggests that the four readings in a group session be done by three different people, with the first reader reading twice. I'm not sure why the first reader would need to read twice, or why four different people instead of three aren't selected to read; maybe it has to do with establishing who the leader of the group is. In any event, having several readers is a good idea, because we hear things in a different way when a different person speaks.

At the end of the time of personal reflection, each member of the group shares what happened during the time of lectio, which is fine if the group members understand from the start that they're not under any pressure to have some fabulous and impressive insight. That misunderstanding would quickly threaten to turn this wonderful spiritual practice into a competition and the participants into active seekers rather than passive listeners.

And remember: this is one way, or maybe two ways, to do group lectio. Feel free to create your own way. Just watch what you call it.

out much later had a well-known Latin name: *lectio divina,* which can be translated "divine reading" or "reading God."

You've probably heard of lectio divina by now. Though it was for a long time unknown in the evangelical world, enough of us are reviving the

Pray and read, read and pray; for a little from God is better than a great deal from men.

—JOHN BUNYAN

practice that it's starting to become a familiar term. Lectio, as it's come to be known, is the subject of many books and chapters in books on the market now, and it would have been so easy for me to pick up only one of those books, take it to be the last word on what lectio divina means and how it's practiced, and then get on with the actual practice of it. But no, I couldn't do that. I had to research it to death, and now I'm convinced that no two people actually agree on what it is. (One of my favorite comments comes from an expert on the Rule of Benedict, which speaks at length of the practice. He writes about various Benedictine disciplines, including "lectio divina, whatever that is." He's being ironic, but it's still a priceless quote.)

Here's what all the sources do seem to agree on: lectio is a way of reading the Scriptures that involves an encounter with God as we listen to what he is saying to us through the text. Even calling it a way of reading the Scriptures is open to debate, though, since many people who practice a form of lectio use books other than the Bible—or more accurately, in addition to the Bible. But most lectio experts contend that using any book other than the Bible is a different practice altogether and should not be confused with lectio.

To spare you the agony of researching lectio to death as I did, and to keep this as simple as possible, I hereby provide you with a bulleted list of the essentials:

- Turn to a portion of Scripture that the Holy Spirit brings to mind. The passage will often stem from your daily reading; a

---

Some read the Bible to learn and some read the Bible to hear from heaven.

—ANDREW MURRAY

few verses will seem to leap out at you, and you will want to
spend more time with them.

- Read those verses over several times, out loud if possible.
  Hearing your own voice utter the words makes them more
  personal to you.

- Ignore any preconceived idea of what the verses mean. This is
  your time to listen to God speaking to you directly, through his
  Word. Isolate a phrase or a sentence in the passage that has made
  a strong impression on your spirit.

- Linger over the phrase. Repeat it slowly, meditatively. Open your
  heart to what the Spirit is saying to you.

- Don't try to analyze the phrase or conjure up your own insight
  into what it means. Rest in the assurance that God will respond
  to your prayerful reading of his Word.

- In this time of quiet attentiveness to God, you'll reach a state
  similar to that of contemplative prayer—a state in which you are
  gently made aware of his divine presence surrounding you.

- Continue to repeat the phrase, maintaining a receptive, listening
  attitude. Even after God has shown you what he wanted to, he
  may have more for you. Your lectio time is over when you sense
  it's over. It usually lasts just a matter of minutes.

- If nothing "happens," if it seems as if God is nowhere to be
  found, so be it. You showed up, you spent time in the Word, you
  listened attentively—you did your part. Now let God do his, in

> *Idleness is the enemy of the soul. And therefore, at fixed times,*
> *the brothers ought to be occupied in manual labor;*
> *and again, at fixed times, in sacred reading.*
>
> —RULE OF BENEDICT

his own time. He may surprise you with an amazing insight into the passage later in the day—or next month. In any event, the time you spend in lectio is never wasted.

Thomas Keating is a leader in the current revival of interest in lectio. He describes one of the results of the practice in this way: "For the moment, we break through the veil of our own ways of thinking. The external Word of God in Scripture awakens us to the interior Word of God in our being." That description certainly rings true for me, given my experience with lectio.

Although lectio divina in its present form was an outgrowth of monasticism, the practice stems from an ancient Jewish method of meditating on shorter passages of the Scriptures. Some of the desert dwellers continued the tradition; John Cassian, the desert journalist, relates an encounter with an elderly desert father named Germanus that has all the earmarks of the practice of lectio. Early Christians in other areas no doubt also practiced a form of prayerful reading like that which came to be known as lectio.

Benedict of Nursia gave lectio its first formal standing in the life of a monastic community in his Rule for Monasteries, better known today as the Rule of Benedict or simply Benedict's Rule. Then, in the twelfth century, a treatise titled *Ladder of Monks* by Guigo II outlined four "steps" that comprise lectio divina: *lectio,* reading the Word; *meditatio,* meditating on it; *oratio,* praying over the Word; and *contemplatio,* contemplating or "being with" God. Calling them "steps" is a bit misleading, since the four elements flow into each other throughout your time spent in lectio.

To read without reflecting is like eating without digesting.

—EDMUND BURKE

Nearly every author who writes about lectio insists that you don't have to worry about doing it the "right" way, but then they go about telling you the right way to do it. So all I'm going to say is: this is one way to do it.

> *Read, mark, learn, and inwardly digest.*
>
> —BOOK OF COMMON PRAYER

Chapter 16

Memorizing the Psalter

O f all the spiritual practices we've inherited from our ancestors in the faith, this may be the biggest challenge for contemporary Christians. Memorizing the Psalter means just what it says—memorizing all one hundred fifty psalms in their entirety. That sounds like a huge undertaking, but many of the faithful who have preceded us considered it to be part of normal Christian living—or Jewish living. You believed in God; you committed the psalms to memory. It was as simple as that.

How did they do it? Maybe a better question is this: Why did they do it? And the best question of all: Why should we?

I'll take a stab at those questions in order. As far as I know, there's no indication that the ancients had a step-by-step Scripture memory plan of any sort that was even remotely related to the kind of thing we see all over the Internet and in Christian bookstores across the land. They didn't have a plan because they didn't need a plan. They heard the psalms recited so often that the Psalter had seeped down into their spirits and found a home there. Maybe I'm wrong about this, but I don't think it was necessary for an observant Jew to sit down with the Psalter and struggle to commit it to memory; from the day he was born, he would have heard the psalms in the synagogue or in the home just about every day of his life. The psalms were originally sung or chanted, and they were sung frequently, one after the other, year after year after year. If you know one hundred fifty songs by heart—and I'm guessing most of us know that many and more—you can see how much easier it would have been to memorize the psalms back when they were routinely sung.

Knowing the psalms by heart was essential to a practicing Jew who wanted to participate fully in corporate worship services and pass his faith along to his family. In his private worship, he would pray the psalms to God as if he, and not David or another psalmist, had written them himself. The first Christians, who were primarily Jews, continued the practice of memorizing, reciting, praying, and meditating on the Psalter—only now, certain psalms took on added meaning as believers recognized evidence in them that pointed to Jesus as the Messiah. Bishops, by the way, were required to memorize all the psalms.

---

*The prophets wrote books, then came our fathers
who put them into practice. Those who came
after them learnt them by heart. Then came the
present generation, who have written them out and
put them in their window seats without using them.*

—ANONYMOUS FOURTH-CENTURY DESERT DWELLER

But some of the early Christians weren't content to stop there; they also memorized the entire New Testament—or rather, whatever portion of it that was available to them, since the New Testament as we know it today had not yet been standardized. All that Scripture memory served them well when wave after wave of official persecution hit the church with full force. The truth they had memorized in Psalm 119:11—"Thy word have I treasured in my heart, that I may not sin against thee" (NASB)—proved its mettle as saint after saint was challenged to renounce his faith and deny God. Some did, but many more did not, often facing death with the words of Scripture on their lips.

Before I get to that third question, I have to say this: threatened persecution is no small motivator when it comes to memorizing Scripture. Those of you old enough to remember Hal Lindsey's *The Late, Great Planet Earth* may also remember the resulting Scripture-memory frenzy. The end was near, and we'd better get ready for it. Prophecies warned that the time was coming when Bibles would be outlawed and confiscated. It could happen tomorrow! Start hiding the entire Bible in your heart tonight!

I'm not sure today how seriously I took those warnings; I did think it was kind of cool that I had emerged from one counterculture—the one associated with Woodstock—only to find myself smack in the middle of another one, the Jesus People Movement. I could even be a martyr in this one! All the talk of impending persecution and the second coming of Jesus

*The LORD was teaching you that people need more
than food to live—
they need every word that the LORD has spoken.*

—DEUTERONOMY 8:3B CEV

Christ fueled my desire to memorize as much Scripture as I possibly could before the Commies came to take away my last Bible, or Jesus came and I would be found unworthy because I hadn't finished memorizing all 176 verses of Psalm 119 yet. Heaven forfend!

So every Monday night, like clockwork, my friend Allen would come to my apartment, where we would spend an hour or two reciting the Scripture verses we had memorized the previous week and helping each other when we got stuck.

Before I go any further, I have to clarify what I mean by "the Scripture verses we had memorized." We did not even consider memorizing isolated verses of Scripture. No way! We memorized large portions of the Bible—entire chapters and entire books. We started by working our way through the book of Psalms in order but then began skipping around and selecting psalms that were significant to each of us personally. After we had memorized a dozen or so psalms, we each chose a book of the Bible to memorize. I can't recall which book Allen chose; I memorized the book of James and still remember most of it today with little prompting.

Things were going along great until we decided to tackle Psalm 119, just to prove that we could do it. At that point, our endeavor crumbled. Instead of memorizing out of a deep desire to hide the Word of God in our hearts, we were attempting to memorize a passage out of pride. No wonder we quit. (Well, we didn't officially quit, but first one of us begged off, and

This is the secret of the Psalms. Our identity is hidden in them.
In them we find ourselves and God. In these
fragments he has revealed
not only himself to us but ourselves in him.

—THOMAS MERTON

then the next week the other one begged off, and that was the end of our Monday night sessions.)

So now to our third question: Why should we—literate twenty-first century Christians—memorize the psalms? I have an answer for that, but only if we get rid of the word *should* and instead ask what value there is for us to memorize the Psalter. Some of the reasons haven't changed down through the centuries. Allowing the Scriptures to seep deep into our spirits and find a home there is just as valuable to our spiritual lives today as it was for our ancestors in the faith. By memorizing the psalms, you'll never find yourself in a situation in which you haven't got a prayer; the songs are a prayer book and songbook rolled into one, as well as a collection of some of the most beautiful, soul-stirring poetry ever written. The psalms are a perfect antidote for the fluff that passes as devotional writing today, some of which I've written; I speak with authority here.

But let's get real. While some people may approach the task of memorizing the Psalter with the same zeal that Allen and I did in the 1970s, many more will have this response: "You've got to be kidding." But I'm serious in encouraging you to take a stab at memorizing a psalm or two beyond Psalm 23. If you've only memorized individual Bible verses in the past, you may be surprised at how much more valuable it is to memorize a larger chunk of Scripture.

Unless you're hopelessly obsessive-compulsive, it's best to begin with a psalm that speaks to you personally or that addresses a situation in your life right now. (If you're hopelessly obsessive-compulsive, you'll begin with

*And do not be conformed to this world, but be transformed
by the renewing of your mind, that you may prove
what is that good and acceptable and perfect will of God.*

—ROMANS 12:2 NKJV

Psalm 1 and work straight through, but I didn't have to tell you that, did I?) Psalm 139 is my all-time favorite and the one I recommend people start with unless they have a clearly identifiable and pressing need in their lives. The thing about Psalm 139, and many other psalms, is that it thrums along beautifully until verse 19, when David lashes out at the enemies of God for the next four verses: "O that Thou wouldst slay the wicked, O God; depart from me, therefore, men of bloodshed. . . . I hate them with the utmost hatred; they have become my enemies" (vv. 19, 22 NASB). He regains his composure in verse 23 and ends the psalm with one of the best-known prayers in the Psalter, the one that begins, "Search me, O God, and know my heart" (v. 23).

So what are we to do with those passages that speak of violence and hatred and disturb our modern-day sensibilities? I've known Christians who ignored those passages and memorized only those portions that appealed to them. For my part, I think selective memorization does a disservice to David and others who lived in an openly violent society and had all the more cause to rely on God for the safety of their lives. I memorize the entire psalm—the good, the bad, and the puzzling—and remind myself to be grateful, first that the biblical writers didn't gloss over the reality of their times and second, that the violent and difficult passages express neither my heart nor the reality I live in. When I pray a psalm back to God, I omit

---

Let the great {Bible} passages fix themselves in our memory.
Let them stay there permanently, like bright beacons, launching
their powerful shafts of light upon life's problems—our own and
everyone's—as they illumine, now one, now another
dark area of human life.

—FREDERICK C. GRANT

those sections; to do otherwise would be dishonest and would not reflect the cry of my heart.

But that's just me. Some women who have experienced truly heinous violence find it nearly impossible to read certain portions of the Bible. I do think God understands that. You do what you can do, when you can do it. If you can't handle the violence, a good and safe place to start is with one of the praise psalms that glorify God, such as Psalms 146, 147, 148, or 150. (Psalm 149 gets a bit vengeful toward the end.)

If you're in the middle of a difficult situation, here are some psalms that address specific circumstances: Psalm 51 for those who are involved in ongoing sin and have finally had enough; Psalm 73, if the specific sin is envy and resulting bitterness; Psalm 32 after you've accepted God's forgiveness; Psalm 37 if you are in despair and long for a sense of God's presence again; Psalm 103 if you seek physical healing. There are so many wonderful psalms that it's a challenge to choose just a few to recommend. But none of the ones I've mentioned are long—though I realize "long" is a relative term—and they're all psalms that I've memorized and found personally meaningful.

I'm sure a lot of people would like me to provide an easy, step-by-step, tried-and-true method for memorizing Scripture, particularly large portions of Scripture, but frankly, I'm not sure such an animal exists. If you are a method-oriented person, the best advice I can give is to search the Internet for a term like "Scripture memory plan" or go to a Christian bookstore and ask for help finding one that will suit your needs; a mega bookstore like

But his delight is in the law of the LORD,
and on his law he meditates day and night.

—PSALM 1:2 NIV

Barnes & Noble is much less likely to have a wide variety of choices, plus you're not likely to find someone who can offer specific help. Personally, I use the Nike plan: "Just do it." Having Allen as a Scripture-memory buddy helped immensely way back when, so find a partner if being accountable to someone helps get you going. But really, there's nothing like constant exposure to a passage of Scripture to help you remember it.

If you do decide to tackle the entire Psalter, you'll have a "great cloud of witnesses" cheering you on, those who have gone before you and successfully committed the psalms to memory. Take a deep breath, ask for God's help and guidance, pace yourself, and get going. You'll never regret undertaking this spiritual exercise, even if you discover along the way that you've taken on more than you feel you can handle. If that happens, just thank God for what you were able to accomplish and treasure the Scripture that you have stored in your heart.

Sometimes the special word is in the portion
you would naturally read, or in the Psalm
for the day . . . but you must go on till you find it,
for it is always somewhere. You will know
it the moment you come to it,
for it will rest your heart.

—AMY CARMICHAEL

Chapter 17

Unceasing Prayer

We really are a peculiar people, we Christians. Some of us will fight to the death maintaining that Hebrews 10:25 is valid today; despite the busyness of our lives, we are expected to attend church services one or more times per week. (That's the verse that warns us not to get out of the habit of meeting with other Christians.) But we find it perfectly acceptable to use that same busyness as an excuse to blithely dismiss Paul's even clearer admonition to "pray without ceasing" (1 Thess. 5:17). Obviously, we rationalize, those words were meant for people who lived in a simpler day and age. The only people today who could possibly pray without ceasing are people in religious orders, the bedridden, and the like.

That kind of thinking is faulty. For those of us who live in a hectic world that is largely of our own making, we not only *can* pray without ceasing but also *need* to pray without ceasing. Our biggest barrier in accomplishing that is the way we think about prayer.

The ancients had no problem with the way they thought about prayer. To the desert dwellers in particular, prayer was not a part of their lives; prayer *was* their lives. "When the Spirit has come to reside in someone, that person cannot stop praying; for the Spirit prays without ceasing in him," wrote Isaac the Syrian, who learned about prayer from the accounts of the desert fathers who lived several centuries before he did. "No matter if he is asleep or awake, prayer is going on in his heart all the time. He may be eating or drinking, he may be resting or working—the incense of prayer will ascend spontaneously from his heart. The slightest stirring of his heart is like a voice which sings in silence and in secret to the Invisible."

It would be tempting to make a neat and tidy list of the various forms prayer can take, but that's the subject for a book and not a chapter, and certainly not a portion of a chapter. Think instead of the general ways you pray now: corporately, with the rest of the body of Christ during church services or with friends and family in more personal settings; privately, during those times you set aside for an intentional conversation with God; and mentally, as you shoot "arrow" prayers—one-liners appropriate to the immediate situation—to God throughout the day.

That pretty much sums up the typical way we think about prayer. We obviously can't practice ceaseless prayer in the first two ways—nor has God called us to do so, at least not most of us. (If you're reading this, you can rest assured you haven't been called to a life of intentional, focused,

---

I pray without ceasing now. My personal prayer is:
Make me an instrument which only truth can speak.

—PEACE PILGRIM

ceaseless prayer. If you were, you wouldn't be reading this or any other book.) Ceaseless prayer most closely resembles the third form, the arrow prayers, but the practice—as I understand it and follow it, anyway—is both more and less than that.

First, unceasing prayer requires a state of mind that is attentive to what is going on *now*. This is where I fall short most often, right here in step number one. Like many people, my mind is constantly whirring with thoughts that have very little to do with what is happening at any given moment. If you have children, you have probably been made aware of your tendency toward distraction more often than you'd like to be; even introverted kids are not shy about letting their parents know that they're not giving them their full attention. My teenager has taken to grabbing my chin and turning my head toward her to force me to focus on what she is saying. And they say mothers induce guilt!

Before I become further distracted, let me continue with a second aspect of unceasing prayer that is helpful to keep in mind: ceaseless prayer works on both a conscious and an unconscious level. We pray on a conscious level as we intentionally express our thoughts and requests to God either aloud or mentally, but we continue to pray on a subconscious level even when our conscious thoughts are elsewhere to the extent that we have prayed on a conscious level and hidden the Word of God in our hearts. See how these practices overlap? If you have memorized the psalms and other portions of Scripture, and if you have developed a fairly disciplined intentional prayer life, your spirit will continue to thrive in a prayerful, open

Pray without ceasing.

—1 THESSALONIANS 5:17 NKJV

attitude toward God even when your conscious thoughts are on the current budget or the next deadline or the cranky neighbor who is right now yelling at your son.

It's on that unconscious level that our very lives become a prayer to God. Even when we are not praying on a conscious level, everything we think, say, and do becomes a prayer to God when our hearts are turned toward him. That's troublesome for a chronic kvetch like me; how can my heart be turned toward God when I'm constantly grumbling? But then again, I'm in good company, what with all the complaints Moses and Jeremiah and even Naomi directed toward the Almighty. In fact, I feel a whole lot better about voicing an honest complaint to God than I would if I expressed a positive sentiment that had no basis in my reality.

But back to unceasing prayer and how to do it. Like just about every spiritual practice, you do it the way that works best for you, but here are some methods to choose from:

1. If you've got a fairly significant stockpile of Scripture deep in your spirit, you can begin immediately to draw on those verses at appropriate moments throughout the day. Start your day by repeating Psalm 118:24 ("This is the day the LORD has made; let us rejoice and be glad in it" HCSB) aloud or in your head as an expression of gratitude to God. Maybe you're like me; gratitude for the day doesn't kick in until I've expressed gratitude for the wonder-working miraculous substance that is the coffee bean; then and only then can I seem to remember to be grateful for another day of life. As I said, you do what works best for you.

> *The desire is your prayers; and if your desire is without ceasing,*
> *your prayer will also be without ceasing. The continuance*
> *of your longing is the continuance of your prayer.*
> —AUGUSTINE OF HIPPO

Throughout the day, look for opportunities to engage in this kind of mental, scriptural prayer. Once you begin doing this, you'll probably discover that there truly is a Bible verse for every occasion, like taking a shower ("Cleanse me from my hidden faults" Ps. 19:12 HCSB) or chatting with friends or coworkers ("LORD, set up a guard for my mouth; keep watch at the door of my lips" Ps. 141:3 HCSB) or taking out the garbage ("Whatever you do, do it enthusiastically, as something done for the Lord and not for men" Col. 3:23 HCSB). When your attention is directed toward unceasing prayer, you'll find that even your Bible reading is being transformed, as you discover new verses to use during specific activities in your day. One woman I know of recites Psalm 139:13 ("For it was You who created my inward parts; You knit me together in my mother's womb" HCSB) whenever she's doing needlework of any kind.

If you don't have that stockpile of Scripture to draw on, you will eventually—because as long as you're reading the Word of God prayerfully and attentively, you will be hiding it in your heart.

2. Some people—both those who are new to the tradition and those who are veterans—practice unceasing prayer by mentally reciting the Jesus Prayer (chapter 2) or another appropriate prayer or phrase throughout the day. In fact, it's often suggested that you use this method when you're first starting to practice ceaseless prayer; it's much easier to train yourself to return to the same phrase over and over again each time your conscious thoughts turn toward something negative. The Jesus Prayer and others

Rejoice in hope; be patient in affliction; be persistent in prayer.

—ROMANS 12:12 HCSB

like it train your mind and your heart to turn back to God whenever you become restless or agitated or troubled in any way.

There's also a different way entirely of understanding the concept of unceasing prayer, and that's to think of the openness of your heart toward God as a continual silent prayer. In other words, as long as your heart is inclined toward God and you are seeking to please God and do His will, as long as you are living in the presence of God and in a state of spiritual attentiveness, then you are in a perpetual state of prayer. Augustine interpreted "pray without ceasing" in this way: "Are we then to ceaselessly bend our knees, to lie prostrate, or to lift up our hands? . . . There is another, interior kind of prayer without ceasing, namely, the desire of the heart . . . . The constancy of your desire will itself be the ceaseless voice of your prayer."

If that's the case, well, I can honestly say that I often pray without ceasing. Otherwise, I'm still in the early training stage. I still have to intentionally remind myself to turn my thoughts back to the prayer I'm supposed to be praying. But then I remind myself that it's all good—that whatever time I spend in prayer is *good.*

Ceaseless internal prayer is a continued yearning of the human spirit towards God. To succeed in this consoling exercise we must pray more often to God to teach us to pray without ceasing. Pray more, and pray more fervently. It is prayer itself which will reveal to you how it can be achieved unceasingly; but it will take some time.

—*THE WAY OF A PILGRIM*

Chapter 18

Manual Labor

L et's face it: many of us do our very best to avoid physical labor. Our
society has moved largely from one in which manual labor was the
mainstay of our ancestors' existence to one in which physical exertion
doesn't even make a blip on the radar screen of the lives of many of us. But
the ancients viewed physical work, whether strenuous or easy, as an opportunity for our lives to become an act of prayer toward God.

For many of the desert dwellers, manual labor was considered a crucial
element of their disciplined lives. They saw work as a sacramental act and
a means of providing for the poor. While some desert fathers and mothers
reportedly spent all their time in prayer and study, others believed that a life
devoted exclusively to religious pursuits denied the sacredness of all of life.
While we think of the desert dwellers as having little but the clothes on

their backs—if that, in the case of some naked ascetics—a fair number had
an extensive library at their fingertips. It's important to remember that the
desert Christians came from all walks of life; some were wealthy, powerful,
and well-educated. Though they kept only what they needed when they
ventured out to the desert, the definition of *need* varied.

As the desert dwellers began to recognize the importance of community and monastic orders came into being, the concept of work as a sacred
activity became more widely accepted. That concept was popularized in
The Practice of the Presence of God, a seventeenth-century compilation of conversations and letters attributed to Brother Lawrence (see p. 132), but the
concept was already a familiar one to both the monastics and the laity.

Monasteries hardly ran themselves; for the most part, the monks
assumed responsibility for the cooking, cleaning, gardening, livestock tend-
ing, sewing, mending, repairing—everything that was involved in keeping
the monastery operating smoothly. Much of their work was repetitive, and
it didn't take long for them to recognize the meditative nature of the work
they did.

Likewise, the laity recognized the sacramental nature of work. As the
Roman Empire crumbled and illiteracy increased, people who might have
been drawn to religious books in a more literate era found spiritual value
in the work of their hands—which is, of course, what the phrase "manual
labor" literally means. The more repetitive the work, the better; mindless
work was transformed into a natural form of meditation.

> *I walk before God simply, in faith, with humility and with love;*
> *and I apply myself diligently to do nothing and think nothing*
> *which may displease Him.*
>
> —BROTHER LAWRENCE

PRACTICING THE PRESENCE AT WORK

One of the books that greatly enriched my life as a new believer was Brother Lawrence's *Practice of the Presence of God.* I understand it on a whole other level now, but even though my comprehension of it as a baby Christian may have been incomplete, it touched my life in a lasting way.

Fortunately for us, Brother Lawrence touched the life of a seventeenth-century French cleric in a lasting way. Brother Lawrence became a Carmelite monk later in life after a career as a soldier and a servant to a public official and was virtually unknown outside his monastic community during his lifetime. After Lawrence died, the cleric published his recollections of conversations with his monastic friend, as well as some of the letters he wrote. Below are excerpts from that compilation:

- In his business in the kitchen (to which he had naturally a great aversion), having accustomed himself to do everything there for the love of God, and with prayer, upon all occasions, for His grace to do his work well, he had found everything easy, during the fifteen years that he had been employed there.

- [He said that] we ought not to be weary of doing little things for the love of God, who regards not the greatness of the work, but the love with which it is performed. That we should not wonder if, in the beginning, we often failed in our endeavors, but that at last we should gain a habit, which will naturally produce its acts in us, without our care, and to our exceeding great delight.

- [And] when he had thus in prayer filled his mind with great sentiments of that infinite Being, he went to his work appointed in the kitchen (for he was cook to the society); there having first considered severally the things

his office required, and when and how each thing was
to be done, he spent all the intervals of his time, as well
before as after his work, in prayer.

- As Bro. Lawrence had found such an advantage in walking in the presence of God, it was natural for him to
recommend it earnestly to others; but his example was a
stronger inducement than any arguments he could pro-
pose. His very countenance was edifying; such a sweet and
calm devotion appearing in it, as could not but affect the
beholders. And it was observed, that in the greatest hurry
of business in the kitchen, he still preserved his recollec-
tion and heavenly-mindedness. He was never hasty nor
loitering, but did each thing in its season, with an even
uninterrupted composure and tranquility of spirit. "The
time of business," said he, "does not with me differ from
the time of prayer; and in the noise and clutter of my
kitchen, while several persons are at the same time calling
for different things, I possess God in as great tranquility
as if I were upon my knees at the Blessed Sacrament."

- As he proceeded in his work, he continued his familiar
conversation with his Maker, imploring His grace, and
offering to Him all his actions.

- When he had finished, he examined himself how he had
discharged his duty; if he found well, he returned thanks
to God; if otherwise, he asked pardon; and without being
discouraged, he set his mind right again, and continued
his exercise of the presence of God, as if he had never devi-
ated from it. "Thus," said he, "by rising after my falls, and
by frequently renewed acts of faith and love, I am come
to a state, wherein it would be as difficult for me not to
think of God, as it was at first to accustom myself to it."

It's ironic that our culture so despises the notion of repetitive work, and yet we suffer from an array of repetitive stress injuries in jobs that in some cases are considered desirable. Could that have something to do with our attitude toward repetitive work? In an earlier time, so-called mindless repetition would have been considered by some to be a blessing. If you didn't have to think about what you were doing, your mind was free to pray or meditate or recite all those psalms you had memorized. Maybe our injuries result more than we realize from our failure to integrate spiritual discipline into our work lives. I'm just speculating about that, but it's a possibility worth considering.

Spiritually oriented women who work in the home have probably always been aware of the connection between repetitious work and meditation. Activities like knitting, ironing, doing the dishes, gardening, vacuuming, and dusting all lend themselves to a meditative frame of mind. As a result, we may at some point realize that we've been praying without being aware of it, or silently blessing the people we're serving through our work, or finding solutions to problems we weren't even consciously thinking about.

I've experienced this process countless times in my adult life. One situation in particular made me a lifelong believer. I was working as a magazine editor at the time and was struggling to find a compelling way to write the introductory paragraphs of the cover feature article for the next issue. I tried this and that to no avail and left on a Friday afternoon facing a Monday deadline. That weekend, as I hosed down the outdoor furniture

---

We labor, working with our own hands.
When we are reviled, we bless;
when we are persecuted, we endure it.

—1 Corinthians 4:12 HCSB

No-No Professions

Though the necessity of work was emphasized in the early church, not all professions were considered appropriate for Christians. In fact, many of us today would be rejected as candidates for baptism if the thinking of the early church fathers regarding careers had survived to our time. Among the forbidden professions listed in Hippolytus's *Church Order* are these:

- Pagan priests or anyone responsible for the upkeep and cleaning of idols.
- Theatrical actors, due to the obscenity and immorality that characterized performances in that day.
- Athletes, gladiators, spectators, and organizers of games that disregarded the safety of the participants and sometimes included intentional killing.

In addition, other occupations were considered suspect, for varying reasons:

- Government employees, because they may at some time be called upon to help organize and participate in pagan activities such as festivals.
- Teachers, because they were forced to teach mythology to their students.
- Artists and sculptors, because they may be required to paint the image of an idol or create idols.
- Soldiers, because they may be ordered to guard pagan temples or kill unjustly. The church automatically rejected as a candidate for baptism any man who took the military oath after seeking baptism; those who were soldiers already were apparently grandfathered in.

in anticipation of the hot weather to come, I was in an unusually prayerful frame of mind. I can't say today what I was subconsciously or even consciously thinking about. All I can say is that my heart was open to God. I was not thinking about that blasted article or the approaching deadline, but right there I solved the problem that was keeping me from getting that article done. Because I was involved in a rare moment of physical labor, the anxious thoughts that normally plague my mind were replaced by a meditative frame of mind that accompanies repetitive work.

"We know we are getting the message stored in the teaching on manual labor when we expect to be asked to do the lowest task and we take it up with preference, for the sake of the spiritual life," writes Mary Margaret Funk in *Tools Matter for Practicing the Spiritual Life*. I'm not quite at that point yet; I suppose I need to allow the teaching on manual labor to sink more deeply into my spirit. I can't say that I prefer the lowest task and expect to be asked to perform it. But I can say this: when I engage in manual labor of my own making, I find it deeply satisfying. After sitting at a desk all day and night, writing and editing and reading and researching, I sometimes welcome the opportunity to do some repetitive physical work. Mind you, I said "sometimes," and I purposely left out the word *strenuous*. Anyone who has seen the condition of our house when I'm neck deep in an editorial project knows the minuscule percentage of time I devote to housework.

Back to Funk's comment on preferring "the lowest task." That would have been unthinkable in an earlier age, when society consisted of nobility

> *A man will be satisfied with good*
> *by the words of his mouth,*
> *and the work of a man's hands will reward him.*
>
> —PROVERBS 12:14 HCSB

and menial workers, with a smattering of scholars and clerics in between. The upper crust considered manual labor to be so far beneath them that work would simply be left undone if there were no one to do it—if, say, the gardener suddenly dropped dead or the maid ran off with the butler. For centuries, though, monks had been quietly performing menial tasks to the glory of God, subtly and slowly altering the way people viewed their work. What the nobility could not see was that engaging in hard work was more noble than whatever it was that the nobility engaged in.

But whether our work is hard or mindless or—miracle of miracles!—completely satisfying, we can allow God to sanctify that work by bringing him into whatever it is we're doing, by praying, meditating, or turning our thoughts toward him. In that process, we continue our ongoing conversation with God—even if our minds need to be actively focused on the task at hand as we engage in manual labor. (We wouldn't want a logger with a chainsaw in his hands to lose his concentration, would we?)

Next time you're chopping vegetables, mowing the lawn, shoveling snow, or folding laundry, open your heart to God, slow down, and either repeat a phrase from your "ceaseless prayer" practice or just meditatively pray appropriately, blessing the people you are cooking for, expressing gratitude that you are healthy enough to mow your lawn, thanking God for the beauty of the snow, asking God to be with those who will wear all those clean clothes. When you see your work as sacred and the tools of your work as gifts from God, everything changes.

Practical prayer is harder on the soles of your shoes
than on the knees of your trousers.

—AUSTIN O'MALLEY

Chapter 19

Prayer Postures

The sign of the cross is still something of a mystery to me. Honestly, somebody ought to corral all us liturgically minded newbies into a separate room and teach us when to sit, stand, kneel, genuflect, make the sign of the cross, and get up to finally go home. I've been confused more than once about when a service was actually over, and not just in liturgical churches.

But back to the sign of the cross, which dates to at least the second century and served a twofold purpose at that time: as a sign of identification with Christ but also as a secret sign of solidarity during the Roman persecution of Christians. Today it's often used at the beginning and end of prayers and at certain times when reciting the creeds. Oh, and at other times too, which is why it's so confusing to newcomers. I just use it in my private prayer and figure it will eventually become second nature to me. By the way, the proper sequence is to touch the forehead, the middle of the torso (near the heart, which is closer to the center of the body than many people realize), the left shoulder, and finally the right shoulder. Those four areas of the body symbolize, in order, the mind, heart, strength, and soul.

One gesture that I've grown to love is not really related to prayer. It's one certain ministers use each time they begin to preach. They place their thumb and forefinger together and make something of a "buttoning" gesture over their foreheads, their lips, and their hearts, symbolizing the consecration of their minds, their words, and their attitudes to God. Sometimes they do it so imperceptibly that you barely realize they've done it—indicating to me, at least, that this is a personally meaningful gesture in their lives. They take the responsibility of the pulpit seriously.

The prayer posture that for me signifies overwhelming adoration and thanksgiving is full and open. From a standing position, supplicants extend their arms outward and upward, offering an abundance of praise to the Lord. I've read where some people see this as a gesture of "getting"—their arms are spread wide open to receive God's abundant blessing. That doesn't resonate with me at all, though it may with you. This gesture, to me, symbolizes giving—giving my all to God, starting with my praise and adoration.

On its own, standing symbolizes the resurrection and our new life in Christ—our new "standing" before God. Just as standing to greet someone

---

The Lord understood that the virtue of the soul is shaped by our outward behavior. He therefore took a towel and showed us how to walk the road of humility {see John 13:4}. The soul indeed is molded by the doings of the body, conforming to and taking shape from what it does.

—JOHN CLIMACUS

is a sign of respect in the secular world, when we stand to pray in church, we are showing respect for the Lord.

There's another raised-hands position called the *orant* position. You see this position often in ancient and medieval art, most commonly in the frescoes that adorn the catacombs in Rome that date through the sixth century. The supplicant stands with arms bent at the elbow and forearms extending upward, forming something akin to the shape of a W. This position puts me in a more reflective frame of mind—or rather, when I find myself using this position, it's because I'm already in a more reflective frame of mind.

The orant position may be similar to the one Moses assumed when the Israelites battled the Amalekites at Rephidim, though Moses did end up having to sit down: "And so it was, when Moses held up his hand, that Israel prevailed; and when he let down his hand, Amalek prevailed. But Moses' hands became heavy; so they took a stone and put it under him, and he sat on it" (Exod. 17:11–12 NKJV). Why it worked this way I have no idea, since scholars seem to disagree on the meaning of this passage. All I'll say is, there must have been a worshipful element to Moses' posture, because God did give the Israelites the victory.

Another standing position is accomplished by forming the shape of the cross with your body, standing with legs together and extending your arms outward to the side. This position was used by desert dwellers sometimes as a means of penance but more often as a means of entering into the suffering of Christ on the cross. When you stand in this position, you will

---

I urge you, therefore, brethren, by the mercies of God,
to present your bodies a living and holy sacrifice,
acceptable to God, which is your spiritual service of worship.

—ROMANS 12:1 NASB

eventually experience all manner of discomfort, pain being the primary result. What you experience will be pointless unless you combine this position with an intentional meditation on the cross, which makes this an appropriate prayer position for Good Friday.

Here are some other prayer postures that are probably familiar to most Christians, along with the reasons why we assume these positions:

- Bowing: Sometimes you make a slight bow from the waist, while at other times you may find yourself doubled-over in prayer. I've found myself in that position more than once, as I was praying from a standing position and was overcome by the double whammy of an acute awareness of God's awesomeness and my own pettiness. It also serves to symbolize our submission to God's will.

- Kneeling: Kneeling is a sign of humility, an acknowledgement of repentance for our sins, and a recognition of the greatness of God. Daniel openly defied secular authorities by continuing to kneel before the Lord, even after a decree had gone out forbidding worship of God: "When Daniel learned that the document had been signed, he went into his house. The windows in its upper room opened toward Jerusalem, and three times a day he got down on his knees, prayed, and gave thanks to his God, just as he had done before" (Dan. 6:10 HCSB). Incidentally, in some churches, worshipers kneel only as a sign of reverence

---

Someone who shows a reverential posture during prayer, by stretching out his hands to heaven as he stands chastely, or by falling on his face to the ground, will be accounted worthy of much grace from on high as a result of these lowly actions.

—ISAAC THE SYRIAN

STANDING WITH CHRIST

Some rituals have become such a part of the fabric of our lives that we seldom think about why we do them. Take standing during service, for instance. Standing to sing just makes sense; you sing better when your diaphragm and lungs aren't all scrunched up. But we also stand at other parts of the service.

In spite of where early Christians lived—remember the impossibility of having a set order of worship in a wide geographical area during the phenomenal church growth of the first few centuries—they still most likely *knew* that every time they stood during a service they were commemorating the resurrection. Not me. All those times I obediently stood, I thought the pastor was just trying to keep me awake.

The desert dwellers considered standing a sacred act and a spiritual discipline that pointed to the resurrection. That's why they stood for hours, even days, at a time. And as far as staying awake is concerned, they didn't need the help of a pastor.

and never as a sign of repentance, since Sunday marks the resurrection—the Lord's and ours.

- Prostration: This is the ultimate posture of repentance. Lying prone with our face touching the floor, we are not only expressing remorse for our sins, we're also made more acutely aware of them. This is the position I assume when I've finally

Then Miriam the prophetess,
Aaron's sister, took a tambourine in her hand,
and all the women followed her with tambourines and dancing.

—EXODUS 15:20 HCSB

reached the end of myself—when I've run out of ways to avoid humbling myself before God and admitting that I can't do this life very well without him. Believe me, I've inhaled more than a few dust mites and carpet fibers over the years. Abram apparently inhaled his share of dirt when God had something to say to him, as Genesis 17:3 indicates: "Abram fell to the ground, and God spoke with him" (HCSB).

Probably the prayer posture that has the most conflicting explanations is also the simplest: the act of joining our hands together in prayer, either with our palms together and fingers intertwined or palms together and fingers extended. Of all the explanations I've heard or read, the one I like most is the following. Back in the days before metal handcuffs, prisoners' hands were tied together with rope or whatever else might be available. The prisoners' joined hands came to symbolize submission to authority, a symbol that I suspect was not lost on persecuted or martyred Christians in the early years of the church. Their joined hands, however, would have symbolized submission to God's authority and not to that of the earthly enforcers of their day. A far more mundane rationale is that by keeping the hands together, adults are less prone to distraction and children are less likely to create a disturbance—that explanation I understand!

Speaking of distractions, eliminating them is also why we close our eyes in prayer. And we bow our heads as a sign of humility. This is contrary to what one Native American shaman stated publicly at a pow-wow I once attended. He announced to the huge crowd—this was one of those touristy

He who does not bow before God will not be able to bear the burden of himself.

—FYODOR DOSTOYEVSKY

events that attracted more hawkers of Indian artifacts than there are genu-ine Indian artifacts—that unlike Christians, Native Americans do not try to hide from God by closing their eyes and bowing their heads. Well! Is it possible that I could have been more offended? I think not! Seriously, I was surprised to hear him say that, since I couldn't imagine such ignorance and why anyone would think that. Which underscores how difficult it can be to truly understand another person's faith and how faulty our perceptions can be—and I speak for myself as well as for him.

Another palms-together explanation comes from the Middle Ages. We've probably all seen historical movies in which a medieval serf would place his hands together and his lord would then place his hands around the serf's. That served as a pledge of loyalty, a symbol that echoes a Christians' pledge of loyalty to the Lord.

And of course, early Christians faced east, the direction of the rising sun and a symbol of the Risen Son, as well as the direction from which Christ will return (see Matt. 24:27). The architects and builders of medi-eval cathedrals followed this tradition; buildings were oriented toward the east, and the priests faced east as they celebrated Mass. This eastward orientation admittedly had its origins among pagan groups and mystery cults that worshiped the sun. But like other traditions rooted in paganism, turning toward the sun was transformed and sanctified by early Christians. God himself referred to the "sun of righteousness": "But for you who fear My name, the sun of righteousness will rise with healing in its wings, and

Then the virgin will rejoice with dancing,
while young and old men {rejoice} together.

—JEREMIAH 31:13A HCSB

you will go out and playfully jump like calves from the stall" (Mal. 4:2 HCSB).

Then there are movements during prayer, such as genuflecting—a single fluid motion of standing, kneeling, standing (as opposed to kneeling for an extended time in prayer); bowing at the waist when the name of Jesus Christ is mentioned in public prayer; and rhythmic swaying. I'm not talking here about the sentimental sway we do in some churches when we sing a particularly sentimental song. What I'm referring to here is the behavior we see in footage of Jews praying at the Wailing Wall in Jerusalem. Swaying is a way of bringing your entire body into the rhythm of the prayer, especially when you're chanting your prayers.

As sacred dancers will readily tell you, their every movement in a liturgical dance is prayer to God. They're trained dancers, but anyone can dance a prayer to the Lord, as David showed us; he danced "with great abandon before GOD" (2 Sam. 6:14 MSG) and credited God with changing "wild lament into whirling dance" (Ps. 30:11 MSG). In Psalm 149:3–4, the psalmist encourages the Israelites to break out into a dance routine: "Let them praise his name in dance; strike up the band and make great music! Why? Because GOD delights in his people, festoons plain folk with salvation garlands!" (MSG). Plain folk—that's us, the fumbling, uncoordinated, untrained folk who have every reason to dance before our Lord, who doesn't care one bit whether we have the talent for it.

Another form of "moving" prayer is prayer walking, which takes on different meanings in different contexts. The one probably most familiar to

Certain thoughts are prayers. There are moments when, whatever be the attitude of the body, the soul is on its knees.

—VICTOR HUGO

many of us is the evangelistic prayer walk. We walk through our neighbor-hood or a poor area in town or an inner-city hot spot for crime, praying for the people who live and work there, asking God to redeem the area, and speaking a blessing over everyone in the vicinity.

But there's another kind of prayer walk, one that is a meditative activ-ity. During this slow, contemplative activity your focus is entirely on God, which is why it's best to take this kind of walk in a rural area or along a trail or any other place where there is no traffic and where you can walk without giving a whole lot of thought to where you're going.

And finally, we come to my absolute, hands-down, all-time favorite prayer position: lying in bed. It's even biblical—check out Psalm 4, verses 4 and 8. Right before sleep is when my mind stands the greatest chance of slowing down, when the room is dark and my eyes are closed and I can shut out all the concerns of my life by turning my attention to God. Granted, I often fall asleep before I've finished praying, but I'm not convinced that's because Satan doesn't want me to pray, as I've often heard Christian teachers say. (What's up with Satan thinking he can muscle in on my conversations with Almighty God, anyway?) No, I'm convinced now that any time I fall asleep praying it's a gift from God, a gift of assurance that he knows my need for sleep. I like to believe he's saying, "I'll take it from here."

Then He led them out as far as Bethany, and lifting up His hands He blessed them.

—LUKE 24:50 HCSB

Chapter 20

Prayer Closet

I n Matthew 6:5–6, Jesus takes the Pharisees (he says "the hypocrites," but we know—and they knew—who he meant) to task once again by criticizing their habit of making a public show of their piety and advises his followers to pray in private, where only God can see them. Here's how *The Message* expresses verse 6:

"Here's what I want you to do: Find a quiet, secluded place so you won't be tempted to role-play before God. Just be there as simply and honestly as you can manage. The focus will shift from you to God, and you will begin to sense his grace."

This verse describes what has come to be known as the prayer closet, which is how the King James Version translated the Greek word describing a small storage area. Today, though, *closet* carries a wide range of connotations—everything from tiny closets in older homes that have hooks on the wall because they are too shallow to accommodate clothes hangers, to walk-in closets that are larger than the average bedroom.

Regardless of how we interpret what Jesus meant by the word *closet,* his larger meaning is unambiguous: we are to find a private place where we can get real before God. It is to be a sacred place, a private sanctuary where you can be alone with God, pouring out your heart to him and listening to him without any consideration of what others may think—whether for good or bad.

In verse 5 Jesus specifically addressed those who try to appear to be more pious than they are by praying in the presence of others; they clearly need to get out of the limelight and let God deal with them in private. At the opposite end of the spectrum are people who are self-conscious or shy, as well as those who live with constant ridicule because of their faith. And then there's everyone in between. In verse 6, Jesus addresses all of the above.

Finding such a place can be a tall order. Some people live in tiny apartments or houses so cramped that they can barely turn around without bumping into someone or something. Students living in dorms or off-campus housing, especially at a secular college, are often hard-pressed to find a quiet place to pray if their roommates don't share their faith—or even if they do. No doubt about it, the people around us can cramp our spiritual style, whether we live in a dorm with roommates or a house with

---

Accordingly, whatever you have said in the dark shall be heard in the light, and what you have whispered in the inner rooms shall be proclaimed upon the housetops.

—LUKE 12:3 NASB

our family. But God gave us the gift of creativity, and we can use that to find a prayer closet of our own.

Your prayer closet can be:

1. *A room in your house.* This is a no-brainer. I suspect that if you have a spare room—I rebuke the spirit of envy that just swept over me!—you've already figured out that you can use it as a private place for prayer. But maybe not. Maybe you never realized how important it is to have your own private sanctuary, so I stand by this suggestion.

   I'm equally certain that many of you have figured out that your bathroom serves multiple purposes. That's the only private space in many a home, and that's where lots of people spend their quiet time with God. A stall in a public bathroom works as well. I've heard some people express the idea that praying in the bathroom dishonors God, but my suspicion is that not praying dishonors him a whole lot more.

2. *An actual closet.* No kidding—some houses have closets big enough to pray in! Imagine that! I used to pray in our small walk-in closet when I really needed to be alone with God and the children were too young to understand that. They would never think to look for me there. (And before you go thinking that I was irresponsible or abusive, I only did that when my husband was at home and could keep an eye on them.)

Enter into the inner chamber of your mind.
Shut out all things save God
and whatever may aid you in seeking God;
and having barred the door
of your chamber, seek him.

—ANSELM

3. *A special corner of a room.* I now have a corner of our bedroom that
    I use as my private sanctuary. Most of the time I'm alone in the
    house during the day and have complete privacy, but at other
    times my family knows that when I'm sitting in the rocking
    chair in that corner, which I've sectioned off with a three-paneled
    Japanese screen, I'm not to be disturbed. They seldom forget
    what that corner represents, what with the little altar I've set up
    and the Bibles and prayer books piled on it.

4. *A special chair in a room.* Maybe you don't even have the luxury
    of your own corner; for many years I didn't either. That's when
    a special chair comes in handy. It doesn't have to be a chair set
    aside only for the purpose of prayer; it can be any old chair in
    the house. But to you, it's special; you know when you sit there
    that you will be spending time with God, no matter what else is
    going on around you. That chair can become a symbolic private
    sanctuary even when privacy is nowhere to be found.

5. *Your car.* Lots of people pray when they're driving, of course,
    but not as many think to pray in their car when it's sitting in
    the garage—motor off, of course. Think about that—isn't that
    a great place to pray? A lot depends on the temperature—you
    couldn't do this in Florida in the summer, which pretty much
    means all year, or Wyoming in the winter—but there are times
    when your car can double as a prayer closet. If you don't have
    a garage, this is probably not such a great idea; one of your

---

*Now in the morning, having risen a long while before daylight, He
went out and departed to a solitary place; and there He prayed.*

—MARK 1:35 NKJV

neighbors may see you deep in prayer and take you for comatose. Those flashing lights and sirens could do a number on your prayer time!

6. *A set of headphones.* People may still interrupt you, but they are less likely to if they see you wearing headphones. They'll think you're listening to music, but what you're actually doing is listening to God. This works particularly well when you want to pray while you're taking a walk.

7. *A cell phone.* I'm not kidding. I used to vent my frustrations to God in the car on my way to and from work by praying with my cell phone to my ear. This was before earphones became widely available and when cell phones were so huge that they could rest on your shoulder. It was great using my phone that way. Other drivers just ignored me, figuring I was having a fight on the phone with my boss, which I sometimes was—with a capital *B*. No one would have suspected that I seldom turned that phone on, cell charges being so outrageously high back then. It was a decoy that gave me the freedom to talk to God without looking as if I was talking to myself.

8. *A private place outside.* If you can find such a place, great! If not, bring those headphones along. Just sit in a park and mentally pray while the world jogs around you. I love to pray outdoors— when conditions are perfect, that is, with the temperature and relative humidity and barometric pressure and insect life all

---

Go and sit in your cell, and your cell will teach you everything.

—MOSES, A FOURTH-CENTURY DESERT MONK

in tune with my spiritual needs. I would make a lousy hermit, assuming hermits live in climate-uncontrolled environments. Oh, and don't forget the roof, depending on the type of building you live in, how safe the roof is, and how safe you feel there. And balconies: people who live in apartments don't always think of their balconies as a private place, but they can be.

9. *Deep within yourself.* This is the classic understanding of "prayer closet"—a place deep inside you where you can shut out all distractions and enjoy time alone with God. When all your other attempts to find a private place have failed, this is the one you can always rely on. Even those who have a separate space for prayer would do well to cultivate the habit of finding that inward place of quiet and rest. It takes time, and it takes regular practice, but it is possible to create a private sanctuary inside yourself—and it's well worth whatever time and practice you need to devote to it.

The ancients had their caves, the monastics have their cells—and we have a wide range of places we can use as a prayer closet. If we take advantage of the creativity God has given us, we can probably all come up with ideas for places we can use as a private sanctuary. In the meantime, we have ourselves, and we can pray without ceasing from our own inner prayer closets.

And when He had sent the multitudes away, He went up on a mountain by Himself to pray. And when evening came, He was alone there.

—MATTHEW 14:23 NKJV

Chapter 21

Going on Pilgrimage

Growing up with the last name of Edwards and in a family with little sense of heritage or interest in ancestry, I felt cheated of an ethnic identity. I'd hear my friends' families talk about places like Italy or Ireland or Germany; their biannual trips back to the old country sounded as much like a pilgrimage as anything else I had ever heard of in real life. Other than that, my only knowledge of pilgrimages came from reading history textbooks, which bored the living daylights out of me.

It wasn't until I visited a shrine in Montreal that I began to realize that Christians still took the experience of pilgrimage seriously. Jews and Muslims I could understand—they were required to go—but Christians? Sure, a trip to the Holy Land, or maybe to Rome, would make a great vacation. But I'd been to a half-dozen cathedrals in France, and it seemed to me that all I saw were tourists. No one seemed particularly holy. And no one looked like a pilgrim, whatever a pilgrim looked like. Then again, I was seventeen and totally self-absorbed. I figured all those crutches propped up against walls at various shrines had been there for hundreds of years at least; no one would go there on a pilgrimage in our own so-cool day and age, it being the sixties and all.

By the time I visited St. Joseph's Oratory in Montreal, I was at least old enough to pay attention and take the tour seriously. So maybe the shrine attracted several million people a year, many of them genuine pilgrims seeking healing and other favors from God, but I figured they were probably all old and stuck in the 1940s. It would be several decades before I gave any serious thought to pilgrimage again.

Throughout most of Christian history, the urge to embark on a pilgrimage consumed many a devout believer. Actually, the first "Christian" pilgrims weren't even Christians, according to those who consider the journey of the magi to be a true pilgrimage. They make a strong case: The magi's lengthy trip was prompted by what for them was a spiritual sign, a bright star that guided them to Bethlehem. Their trip was clearly a sacred journey; their destination was the birthplace of a baby they would honor as a king and worship as God.

The first Christians were well acquainted with pilgrimage even before they encountered Jesus. As Jews, they knew what every Jew knew:

Stand by the roadways and look.
Ask about the ancient paths:
Which is the way to what is good?
Then take it
and find rest for yourselves.

—JEREMIAH 6:16 HCSB

that the law of Moses required them to be in Jerusalem each year for three major feasts—Passover and the Feast of Unleavened Bread; Pentecost, the Feast of Weeks; and Succot, the Feast of Booths. Jewish men (women were optional) living outside the city were thus required to make a pilgrimage to the city for these observances. It was only natural for the early Christians to make a pilgrimage to Jerusalem.

The earliest surviving accounts of pilgrimages to the Holy Land attest to the fact that Christians made sacred journeys to the area dating back to apostolic times. Jerusalem and the surrounding villages in Palestine where Jesus lived and ministered attracted pilgrims from as far away as Britain and India.

While several specific pilgrimages are mentioned in historical documents, such as Eusebius's account of a bishop's pilgrimage from Cappadocia in present-day Turkey to Jerusalem in AD 217, none that I know of are as detailed or as charming as the account of a three-year pilgrimage taken by a woman now known as Egeria sometime around the fourth century, give or take a century or two. Traveling with companions and several "holy guides," Egeria traced the route of the Israelites through the wilderness, spent considerable time in Jerusalem, and left an extensive record of the liturgy used by the church in Jerusalem. She addresses her account to her "sisters" or "ladies," depending on the translation you're reading, and that account is exquisitely detailed. Maybe that's why I like it so much, or maybe it's because it's believed to be the oldest known formal writing by a woman.

> *For in their hearts doth Nature stir them so,*
> *Then people long on pilgrimage to go,*
> *And palmers to be seeking foreign strands,*
> *To distant shrines renowned in sundry lands.*
>
> —*THE CANTERBURY TALES,* GEOFFREY CHAUCER

Eventually, attitudes toward pilgrimage started to change. Augustine was among the first Christian leaders who voiced the opinion that there was no purpose in visiting the Holy Land since God was with us no matter where we are. By then, though, the church had enough martyrs and enough other holy places that the Holy Land was only one of numerous pilgrimage destinations. Which is one reason why pilgrimage was rejected by Protestants for several hundred years following the Reformation: a thousand-plus years of church history had resulted in so many excesses and so many abuses connected with pilgrimage that the entire concept was dismissed as irrelevant and unnecessary, if not heretical.

It wasn't until the twentieth century that Protestants began returning to the Holy Land in significant numbers, and now it seems nothing can keep them away. Visit any of the major Christian portals on the Internet, and you'll be inundated with ads touting Holy Land tours geared toward Christians. Call me a spoilsport, but my idea of pilgrimage isn't sitting on a tour bus with fifty other people wearing "Jerusalem" T-shirts and chattering away with each other while a tour guide rattles off his spiel into a microphone. That's tourism, not pilgrimage.

Then too, few twenty-first-century Christians will ever take the kind of pilgrimage the ancients and medievals took. Theirs were replete with hardship and danger. Reaching your destination was a sign that God wanted you to be there. There have always been highway robbers and wild animals ready to pounce on travelers, but in medieval times those dangers

Divert my eyes from toys and trinkets,
invigorate me on the pilgrim way.

—PSALM 119:37 MSG

were compounded by the presence of sworn enemies. The Crusades had not exactly made Christians a popular lot outside of Western Europe.

Plus, there was the terrain. We fly right over it, but a pilgrim like Egeria, who must have been hale and hardy and wealthy enough to undertake a three-year pilgrimage, faced an unforgiving and inhospitable landscape on the journey. She writes in detail about climbing the mountains mentioned in the biblical account of the Israelites' time in the wilderness, and people who know those mountains confirm her description: there are no switchbacks, no easy routes up the slopes of some of the mountains she names. It's pretty much straight up and straight down. Accomplish an undertaking like that on a spiritually motivated journey, and I'd say you've had an authentic pilgrimage experience.

There was a time when I would have loved to take the kind of journey Egeria experienced. As a new Christian in the early 1970s, I couldn't imagine anything more wonderful than walking where Jesus walked. I'm sure it's an intensely spiritual experience. But I never seriously considered going on a pilgrimage until the little matter of my ancestry was at least partially resolved, and that only happened in recent years. Until then, I knew nothing about either side of my family beyond a generation or two back. And then I discovered that a grandfather with a bunch of "greats" in front of his name had been an Anglican vicar in a Canterbury parish.

Suddenly, I had a pressing mission in life: I had to go to Canterbury. My resulting trip to Great Britain was an eight-day pilgrimage to the cathedrals of London and the south of England capped off by a one-day trip

A pilgrim is a wanderer with purpose.

—PEACE PILGRIM

north to Liverpool. I expected to return with a Canterbury tale of my own and satisfy a decades-old desire to visit the home of my first teenage love, the Beatles. I called the trip my Rock 'n' Ritual Tour.

I was prepared to experience the breathtaking awe of Westminster Abbey and St. Paul's Cathedral in London, plus Canterbury Cathedral and the ruins of St. Augustine's Abbey. There was also a magnificent cathedral in the once-grimy city of Liverpool that would have been well worth visiting even if the Beatles hadn't been such a big draw. I envisioned moments of heart-stirring bliss as I basked in the wonder of the places where monarchs and saints and, yes, even murderers and scurrilous politicians had left their mark over the centuries.

But while my expectations ran fairly high, nothing prepared me for the sense of *home* that I experienced in Canterbury. There was probably more than a hint of the power of suggestion going on there, but still, as I sat in the Canterbury Cathedral archives researching my dearly departed Grandpa Perkins, I felt genuinely grounded and anchored to a *place* for maybe the first time ever.

That, to me, is what true pilgrimage is—going home. Not to the place where you were born or spent your formative years, but to a place that marks your spiritual home, a place that enhances your own understanding of God. For me, it happens to be a place where I have never lived and where I have no desire to live, in geographical terms. But in visiting Canterbury, I felt as if my life as a Christian had come full circle. To discover that there

*I have also established My covenant with them,
to give them the land of Canaan, the land of their
pilgrimage, in which they were strangers.*

—Exodus 6:4 NKJV

was an Anglican vicar in my lineage, and then to visit the area where he ministered—well, that was almost too much for me to handle.

Pilgrimage doesn't have to involve a significant investment in time or money. Granted, my experience in Canterbury was like no other. But visiting the church in Georgia that was built by Grandpa Perkins's descendants was every bit as much of a pilgrimage. I didn't go there as a visitor; I didn't even go there as his biological descendant. I went there as his spiritual descendant, to restore some sense of connection with what was apparently a devout line of ancestors and the legacy they passed along to me.

If a pilgrimage represents our quest for our heavenly home—which of course it does—then it stands to reason that your destination needn't be a great cathedral or the Holy Land or even a small country church. It doesn't even have to be what we normally think of as a spiritual landmark.

Even better, you don't necessarily have to have a destination in mind at all. The mind, after all, is what sets you off on your journey. From the start, a true pilgrimage is a sacred act of the heart. I'll forgo the temptation to use the phrase "follow your heart," since that's not only a cliché but also an over-sentimentalized one. So I'll just say this: you're on solid ground anytime you go where the Spirit leads you. Even if you have no idea where your pilgrimage will take you, the Holy Spirit will help you find the home you seek.

Religion points to that area of human experience where in one way or another man comes upon mystery as a summons to pilgrimage.

—FREDERICK BUECHNER

Chapter 22

Night Watches

About the only disappointment I experienced the first time I stayed at a monastery was learning that the monks did not observe the dreaded 3:00 a.m. prayer ritual. That's right—I was disappointed. I had looked forward to entering a darkened, cavernous church in the middle of the night and quietly observing the monks lighting the candles that would offer the only illumination for this, the night watch. The night watch—a time when a few Christians would willingly forgo their sleep to maintain a spiritual vigil by worshiping God while their brothers and sisters slept.

I have long loved the silence and solitude that late night affords. Early on in my life as a follower of Christ, I discovered—purely out of necessity—the truly awesome wonder of spending time with God at what I would have once considered an ungodly hour. I had just been promoted to a position on the early morning desk at the newspaper where I worked, which meant mine would be among the last eyes to double-check the paper for errors before it went to press. That also meant my eyes had to be clear and my mind had to be alert by the time I arrived at work at 4:00 a.m.

At first, that wasn't so difficult to accomplish, since I was neurotic about getting to work on time and perfectionistic once I got there. After a while, though, the shine wore off, and I found it increasingly difficult to feel truly alert at such an early hour—or was it late? I decided I needed to get up even earlier than necessary, and without giving it much thought at all, I began spending time with God when I arose rather than when I went to bed, as had been my habit.

From the very first night, I was amazed at how different—how utterly *reverent*—it felt to worship God in the 2:00 a.m. stillness. An incredible, breathtaking hush seemed to surround me, as if God himself were whispering, "Shhh . . . listen . . . there's something significant happening here. The others are at rest. You are here with me, standing in their place." In the quiet of the night, my prayer life and Bible reading were both transformed.

Only in retrospect did I realize this, of course. Without any conscious effort on my part, my prayers became filled with praise and adoration of

---

Meditate on Jacob's wrestling with the angel all night:
be thou also importunate with God for a blessing, and give
not over till he hath blessed thee. . . . Meditate on the agonies
of Christ in the garden, his sadness and affliction all that night;
and thank and adore him for his love, that made him suffer
so much for thee; and hate thy sins which made it necessary
for the Son to suffer so much.

—JEREMY TAYLOR, *HOLY LIVING*

ANCIENT NIGHT OWLS

- Piamon the Virgin was an Egyptian ascetic known for keeping vigil night after night; like many other ascetics who considered it their calling to stay alert during the night as spiritual guardians over those who slept, Piamon believed her mission in life was to remain in prayer all night in anticipation of Christ's hoped-for return in the morning.

- Macrina, a sister of Gregory of Nyssa, a fourth-century bishop, regularly rose in the middle of the night to pray. Her "Psalter was her constant companion, like a good fellow traveler that never deserted her," Gregory wrote of her in *Life of Macrina*. A woman who had grown up accustomed to luxury, Macrina joyously embraced the ascetic life with all its hardships. "Nothing was left but the care of divine things and the unceasing round of prayer and endless hymnody, coextensive with time itself, practiced by night and day," according to Gregory. She frequently spent the entire night in prayer, and on one occasion, the healing of a tumor in her mother's body was attributed to Macrina's all-night vigil on her behalf.

- Pachomius, a fourth-century ascetic, was the founder of the first highly organized and disciplined monastery. Learning how to live the ascetic life under the tutelage of his mentor,

When, on my bed, I think of You,
I meditate on You during the night watches.

                 —PSALM 63:6 HCSB

Palemon, Pachomius had a rough time at first getting the hang of staying awake during the night watches. He had so much difficulty with this that Palemon forced him to carry heavy buckets of sand during the night offices. But he diligently trained himself to remain alert during the night, and according to some accounts, he went for fifteen years without once lying down.

• Our old desert friend Antony was another night owl, frequently pulling all-nighters with the fervor of a college freshman facing a final exam in the morning. When he did sleep, it was often on the bare ground, though on occasion he allowed himself the luxury of sleeping on a mat woven from rushes. His sleep was not always restful, though; Antony was often awakened in the night by demons and "seducing spirits" that sometimes, but not always, came in the guise of an alluring woman. "Again they are treacherous, and are ready to change themselves into all forms and assume all appearances," Antony said. "Very often also without appearing they imitate the music of harp and voice, and recall the words of Scripture. . . . They arouse us from our sleep to prayers; and this constantly, hardly allowing us to sleep at all."

Consider, my son, that my diet is only bread and salt:
I drink no wine, use no oil, watch one half of the night,
spending that time in singing psalms or in meditating on the holy
scriptures, and sometimes pass the whole night without sleeping.

—PALEMON, A FOURTH-CENTURY DESERT FATHER

God and with intercessory requests for others. It just seemed to happen naturally; my mind wasn't fully awake when I began to pray, and so my thoughts weren't consumed with my own needs. In a word, my prayer requests had become pure because they were focused on just about everything but me. I guess I was still asleep, and so I was pretty much out of the way.

I also became aware of how David may have felt as he worshiped God during the night while he tended his sheep. I began to read the psalms with a newfound appreciation for the poetry that must have welled up in his spirit as he sat under the night sky, trusting God for protection, marveling at his creation, and expressing his love and gratitude to him. (I cannot explain why, but my expressions of gratitude to God never feel more authentic than they do in the middle of the night.)

In ancient times maintaining a nighttime vigil was par for the course in certain occupations, such as shepherding, which required one man's attention all night, and guarding the city from a watchman's position on the wall, which involved a three-man rotation in ancient Israel before the Romans took over and established four night watches. It was only natural for a man of faith to turn his thoughts and heart toward God while doing his job in the dark and quiet of the night, regardless of how long or short his particular watch lasted.

Ascetics took to this practice with all the zeal of a true believer. The men and women of the desert had taken to the desert precisely for the purpose of confronting Satan and his band of demons; when better to expect

At night I remember my music;
I meditate in my heart, and my spirit ponders.

—PSALM 77:6 HCSB

them to appear than under cover of darkness? They considered it their sacred duty to remain vigilant while the rest of their world was peacefully sleeping. You can imagine someone like John the Baptist, who was clearly an ascetic, challenging the demons to show themselves so he could single-handedly take them on.

When the church moved away from the desert and the private homes and into designated church buildings, more and more rituals were added, and all-night vigils became commonplace. In the Eastern Orthodox tradition, for example, we know that by the eighth century all-night vigils, attended by both men and women of all ages, were held every Friday night in honor of Mary and on the eves of major feast days. Even earlier, public vigils in honor of martyred Christians were held in Western churches, while private vigils were held at the martyrs' graves. In time, however, women were advised not to participate in cemetery vigils and to keep their daughters with them at all times during the public vigils, due to the very real dangers they faced.

Throughout Christian history, though, individual believers have felt the need to commune with God during the night. Many people have attested to the fact that God, in that charming way of his, has often kept them from sleeping and kept after them until they either got out of bed and began praying or stayed in bed and began praying. Either way, sleep did not come until their time of prayer had run its course.

To further underscore how charming he can be, God also delights in waking people up from a perfectly sound sleep to get them to spend time

> *I would sleep but an hour a day, and that sitting;*
> *and again I would rise up as if I had never slept.*
> *And although I slept, yet my heart was vigilant.*
>
> —JOHN OF MOLDAVIA, A NINETEENTH-CENTURY
> EASTERN ORTHODOX MONK

with him. When he pulls that one on me, my first instinct is to ask, "Can't we do this in the morning?" But more often than not, he jolts me awake with a particular name or situation that I can't ignore. There I am, having that same dream about all these rooms in my house that I've just discovered and I can't figure out how I could have missed them for so many years. Even in my dream I know this has something to do with all those hidden talents and treasures God has blessed me with but I'm too distracted to recognize and all I want is for just one night to have a nice little dream in which my furry little animal friends scamper about a sun-dappled forest as my feathered little bird friends chirp overhead, and then God wakes me up with a loud and clear "Hannah."

I don't have a friend named Hannah, but bear with me and you'll soon see why I'm using a phony name here. Now maybe I haven't talked to "Hannah" in years, and the last time we talked all was well in her world. So I don't know why God used Hannah's name for this 3:00 a.m. wake-up call, but I'm pretty certain it has nothing to do with the wife of Elkanah and mother of Samuel. So I start praying for Hannah, not having a clue why, but the next day Hannah calls out of the blue to tell me her lousy, rotten, cheatin' husband finally left last night and moved in with one of his girlfriends. Hence, the Hannah wake-up call.

That's not exactly an all-night vigil, but I figure a 3:00 a.m. wake-up qualifies for the last watch of the night according to the Roman way of doing things, so it's still a night watch.

I am awake through each watch of the night
to meditate on Your promise.

—PSALM 119:148 HCSB

In addition to all-night vigils at church and private night watches at home, there are all-night prayer vigils with a small group, which I happen to love. I used to be the leader of a youth group that attracted ten to twelve kids on a regular basis, but there was always a core of three or four girls that I knew I could count on to be at every meeting and activity we had. Sure enough, on the night of our first scheduled vigil, those were the girls who showed up. At this and subsequent vigils, I saw the same pattern emerge. We'd start out all gung-ho, mellow out a bit around 1:00 a.m., get truly giddy an hour or so later, mellow out again, and then get wonderfully reflective an hour or so before daylight. Those last few hours were always precious to me, as I watched these young girls express the depth of their hearts in the stillness of the night.

We have so much to gain when we revive an ancient tradition like this, even when we do so only sporadically and with the modifications we need to make in order to make it work. A household in which every member is of one accord is truly a rarity today, and family members aren't always willing to make the necessary sacrifices that would enable another family member to have the space and privacy for an all-night vigil, let alone the peace and quiet during the night or when sleep becomes mandatory the following day.

To modify this practice, try staying up as late as possible or rising much earlier than you normally would. The idea is not to deprive yourself of sleep, though there's something to be said for that; the idea is to stand

---

For a thousand years in Your sight are like yesterday
when it passes by,
or as a watch in the night.

—PSALM 90:4 NASB

guard over your own heart and soul, over your family and friends, over your community, at a time when others are not maintaining spiritual vigilance. Most of all, though, the idea is to spend undistracted time with God in the still and quiet darkness of the night.

> *It was a night of vigil in honor of the LORD, because He would bring them out of the land of Egypt. This same night is in honor of the LORD, a night vigil for all the Israelites throughout their generations.*
>
> —EXODUS 12:42 HCSB

Chapter 23

Christian Meditation

There was a time not so long ago when the word *meditation* was nearly anathema in Christian circles, which may seem odd considering the number of times the word appears in the Bible. But the time was the 1960s and 1970s, and it seemed as if interest in Eastern religions was out of bounds for Christians. Church leaders justifiably saw those faiths as a threat to Christianity, partly because young people in particular were trading in their disenchantment with the church for the exotic appeal of Islam, Hinduism, Taoism, and Buddhism. (Yes, I know—Buddhism is not a religion but a way of life. Or so they say.)

What's more, church leaders saw Eastern *practices* as a threat to committed Christians, and no practice was considered to be as great a threat as Eastern meditation was. Unsuspecting Christians might not understand the dangers of the "mind-emptying" meditation that other religions advocated. That brand of meditation left a person open to who knows what kind of demonic influence. Christian meditation, grounded in the Bible, was the only form of meditation that could stave off demonic efforts to infiltrate the mind and spirit. Ironically, instead of beefing up the emphasis on Christian meditation, the church railed so much against meditation in general that this age-old practice fell into disuse within a significant segment of the church.

If the countless hours of research I've done on ancient practices have taught me anything, it's this: Fear is a thief and a deceiver. Fear convinces us that what we have allowed ourselves to be robbed of wasn't all that valuable to begin with, so we fail to track down our once-cherished possessions and reclaim them for ourselves. Or we take our sweet time doing it. Thirty years is long enough—too long. It's time we restored to the church the practice of meditation as an intentional spiritual exercise, on a much larger scale than it exists now. (Certainly, many Christians continued to meditate over the years, and Christians who have come into the fold in recent years are likely unaware of the ruckus Eastern religions caused.)

The single element that sets Christian meditation apart from Eastern meditation is the Bible. Its Scriptural basis also distinguishes Jewish meditation from that of other traditions. The Israelites' practice of meditation was based in large part on Joshua 1:8: "Do not let this Book of the Law depart from your mouth; meditate on it day and night, so that you may be careful to do everything written in it. Then you will be prosperous and

> *I will reflect on all You have done*
> *and meditate on Your actions.*
>
> —PSALM 77:12 HCSB

successful" (NIV). The Israelites tried to obey these words literally—when they weren't rebelling against God, that is—by "muttering" their meditation. They gave voice to the words of Scripture as they meditated on them, believing not only that they were obeying God but also that hearing Scripture in their own voice would help them recall it better. That, in turn, would help them "be careful to do everything written in it," which was the point of meditation to begin with. They knew that words without action were meaningless.

Throughout our history, Christians have meditated on the Bible in order to draw closer to God. Unlike Bible study, meditation involves taking a short portion of Scripture and spending time with it; I like to think of it as "dwelling" on the verse or verses. If you are beginning to think this sounds like lectio divina, you're right. The difference is twofold: you can meditate without doing lectio (but not vice versa), and your mind can be a bit more active during meditation than during lectio, which is essentially a passive exercise. Your mind isn't fully engaged during meditation, though; you don't want to waste precious time in meditation thinking things through too much.

When you meditate, you search out what God is saying to you through the passage and pursue its truths in a prayerful way. This slightly elevated cognitive and intentional thinking level is also what sets meditation apart from contemplation, which is simply "being" in the presence of God. But for meditation to be truly effective, the thoughts of our mind need to sink down deep into our spirit until they become the meditation of our heart: "May the

Meditation is the life of the soul; action, the soul of meditation; and honor the reward of action.

—FRANCIS QUARLES

words of my mouth and the meditation of my heart be pleasing in your sight, O LORD, my Rock and my Redeemer" (Ps. 19:14 NIV).

Concentrated breathing is important in meditation, as it is in most of the spiritual practices we've looked at. The ancients must have learned early on that the mind cannot slow down unless the body cooperates and even leads the way. A few minutes of deep breathing will bring you into a meditative frame of mind more than anything else I know of.

In addition to meditating on the Bible, you can also meditate on a symbol that has emerged from the Bible, such as the cross or a painting that depicts biblical truth in some way. And since God is the Creator, it's also perfectly acceptable to meditate on God while fixing your eyes on an element in the physical world to allow you to worship the Creator through his creation.

An additional form of meditation is biblical visualization—putting yourself into a story or a scene from the Bible and allowing God to reveal his truth to you as you "live" in that setting. For example, place yourself in the context of Luke 24:13–35—one of my favorite Gospel passages, the walk to Emmaus. Imagine yourself as one of the dejected followers of Christ walking the seven miles from Jerusalem to Emmaus three days after the Crucifixion. You are still in shock from the events of the Friday before; the teacher you loved so much, the one you had placed so much trust in, was executed on a cross between two common criminals. As you and your companion mourn with each other and talk about what has happened, a stranger joins you and asks what you are discussing. Immerse yourself in

I will meditate on Your precepts
and think about Your ways.

—PSALM 119:15 HCSB

that scene, and take it from there—walking along as the stranger speaks, urging him to stay the night at your house so you can continue to hang on his every wise word, and then recognizing him as Jesus as he breaks bread with you. Your heart should begin burning within you the way the hearts of Cleopas and his friend burned within them.

Evangelicals have had justifiable problems with visualized meditation due to the improper use of imagination. But God created our imagination, and God can sanctify our imagination. Francis de Sales, who lived at the turn of the seventeenth century, was a bishop who believed spiritual practices could be entrusted to the laity. He said this: "By means of the imagination, we confine our mind within the mystery on which we meditate, that it may not ramble to and fro, just as we shut up a bird in a cage or tie a hawk by his leash so that he may rest on the hand."

Images of hawks on leashes aside, Francis saw the imagination as a restraint on the mind; by restricting our imagination to a biblical story or symbol, we can focus our attention on that one thing while allowing our imagination to roam freely within that confined environment. The intention is to dwell in the reality of that environment, discover the truth the story or symbol holds for us, and be transformed to the likeness of Christ as a result.

Where there is charity and wisdom, there is neither fear nor ignorance. Where there is patience and humility, there is neither anger nor vexation. Where there is poverty and joy, there is neither greed nor avarice. Where there is peace and meditation, there is neither anxiety nor doubt.

—FRANCIS OF ASSISI

An essential component of meditation is reflection: thinking deeply about how the experience of meditation and the insights you gleaned from it affect you personally. *The Renovaré Spiritual Formation Bible* defines meditation as "prayerful rumination upon God, his Word, and his world." I've always loved that word *rumination;* it carries the idea of a cow chewing the cud, over and over again. That's what we're to do—chew on the Word and the truths of God and let them sink down deeply within us.

Eastern meditation? I think not. We've got a good thing going here; let's not lose it.

Help me understand
the meaning of Your precepts
so that I can meditate on Your wonders.

—Psalm 119:27 HCSB

Chapter 24

Prayer of Examen

As you can probably guess, this tradition involves examination. So why not call it that? I chose not to after reading Richard Foster's definition of the Latin root for *examen,* which carries with it the idea of "an accurate assessment of the true situation." Foster has done more to revive this ancient practice than anyone since Ignatius of Loyola incorporated it into his monumental work, *Spiritual Exercises,* in the sixteenth century.

Foster sees the prayer of examen as a twofold process—reviewing the day (or the hour, the week, the year) with regard to our conscious awareness of God and our response to him, and examining our conscience over the same time period to determine what actions or attitudes we need to repent of and ask God to forgive so that we may continue to be transformed to his likeness. The examen of consciousness precedes and leads to the examen of conscience.

Let me illustrate how this works in real life, at least in my little world. Just yesterday several crummy things happened in our family—not horrible, in the overall scheme of things, but crummy. My daughter found out that a number of the college credits she earned can be transferred to the college she now wants to attend, but those same credits cannot be applied toward her eligibility for financial aid—this, in the middle of a family-wide financial crisis. This same daughter found out that the person she was paying to care for her cats while she's in a housing transition has been neglecting and possibly abusing her cats. And then the receptionist who works for my favorite doctor—I have seven specialists, but who's counting?—called to notify me that the office is no longer accepting our insurance. With seven doctors, I do tend to rate them, and this is the one I would trust my life with. The family-wide financial crisis forced me to cancel my appointment with him and trudge off in search of someone to take his place.

Oh, and while I was out running errands, I went to the Taco Bell drive-thru because it was the only fast-food place with no cars in line, and all I wanted was a drink. Completely unaware of our family-wide financial crisis, the cashier at the window handed my drink to me and waved me off when I tried to pay. It's a good thing, because I realized later that I didn't have enough money on me to pay for the size I ordered, which is pretty crummy.

O LORD, You have searched me and known me.

—PSALM 139:1 NKJV

So now. During my nightly examen of consciousness, I would review everything that happened during the day, not just the lowlights and highlights I mentioned above. I'd look at everything in terms of how aware I was of God's presence as the day unfolded and how alert I was to whatever he was trying to tell me. I have to tell you, sometimes it feels like he's telling me that he doesn't like me a whole lot, but I've learned to get past that kind of thinking pretty quickly. By reflecting on my day in this way, I stop and consider the things that happen from a variety of angles and not just from my own self-centered perspective.

Yes, I think it is unfair that my daughter's credits can't be applied toward financial aid; that just means we'll have to be creative in finding an alternative way to pay for next semester's tuition. The situation with the cats can't continue; as much as I don't want them here in our house, I know they need to be removed immediately from the place where they are and brought here temporarily. And maybe God knows something I don't know about my health, and my former doctor wasn't the best person to handle the problem.

And Taco Bell? God was just showing me that he likes me after all.

During the examen of conscience that follows, I tend to get real, really real—on this day, about my rotten attitude toward all those crummy things that happened. And you know what? I realize that I didn't fare so poorly after all! That's only because I remembered to invite God into the process, though. Without him, examen would be little more than self-abasing introspection—that "I'm the scum of the earth and always will

---

Nothing will make us so charitable and tender to the faults of others,
as, by self-examination, thoroughly to know our own.

—FRANÇOIS FÉNELON

be" kind of thinking. But God reminds me that although I did get a bit, shall we say, miffed throughout the day, I also turned to him for wisdom regarding the tuition problem, showed a rare measure of compassion toward the feline world, and took advantage of an unusual opportunity to ask my doctor's receptionist to convey to him how much I have valued the care he has given me. So I'm not the scum that I thought I was! I sure like having God along during this examen time.

Examen ends with gratitude toward God, which it's highly unlikely you'll forget to express given the gentle way he has of correcting us when we actively seek his correction. It's so much better, I've learned, to seek his correction through the regular practice of examen than to be smacked upside the head because I wasn't paying attention.

As an aid to practicing examen, Foster recommends meditating on the Lord's Prayer or the Ten Commandments (he's borrowing from Martin Luther here), or keeping a journal for people who are inclined toward that activity. Many people aren't, and it bugs me when we're told that we need to keep a journal. After writing all day, just about the last thing I feel like doing is writing even more, and people who never write at all shouldn't be made to feel as if it is an essential way to express their faith. So there.

You can no doubt see the long-term value in the exercise of examen. It may not be fun, but it helps us immeasurably in discerning what needs to change in our thoughts, emotions, attitudes, and actions. Do this enough times, and pretty soon you become conscious throughout each day of how

Examine your motives, test your heart, come to this meal in holy awe.

—1 CORINTHIANS 11:28 MSG

a particular situation is going to shake out when you get into your examen time that night. That will set you straight right away and maybe even keep you from snapping at the clerk in Customer Disservice who can't seem to get it through his thick skull that I want a refund and not a credit on my nonexistent account and who insists on asking me for the account number on an account I don't have and who really needs to go back to school to learn basic communication skills and who also could use a few tips on dental and bodily hygiene. But I digress.

Ignatius believed that by reflecting on our consolations—those things that cause our measure of faith, hope, and love to grow—as well as our desolations—those things that disconnect us from a life of faith, hope, and love—we can discover those areas of our lives where we want to invest our time and spiritual energy. Ignatius also developed a method for practicing examen while on retreat or in a monastic environment. I'd say that unless you're cloistered in some way, shape, or form, you're probably not likely to follow this pattern: (1) examine your shortcomings in the morning so you can be sure to correct them throughout the day; (2) ask God to help you recall the number of times you committed a particular sin on an hour-by-hour basis and then resolve not to commit the sin in the future; and (3) repeat step 2, only this time allow yourself to spend time in genuine remorse over the sin—and then compare your sins today with those of yesterday and last week. Ignatian experts tell me that Ignatius

---

I presuppose that there are three kinds of thoughts in me: that is, one my own, which springs from my mere liberty and will; and two others, which come from without, one from the good spirit, and the other from the bad.

—IGNATIUS OF LOYOLA, *SPIRITUAL EXERCISES*

never intended for people to wallow in their sinfulness and always saw the Christian life as a process of growth and not a pursuit of perfection. Some of his language and methods don't translate well to contemporary ears, they say; he's really not as legalistic as he appears to be. Okay. I'll buy that.

There are a couple of danger zones when it comes to examen. One is the area of unhealthy introspection. This should not be an excruciating, exacting exercise. There's no need to place each moment of the day under a microscope, just as there's no need to go looking for trouble where there is none. Imagine Jesus walking with you throughout your day. Would he point out every petty little thing you were doing wrong? I think not. Be careful not to carry this self-examination too far. Remember, examen provides "an accurate assessment of the true situation"—not a test of your ability to discover just how wicked you really are.

A second danger zone is the area of harsh self-judgment. So maybe you did some things that were so bad that not even I would do them. We're just pretending here, OK? Even so, even so, the point here is to get you past the situation by having you recognize it and confess it and then accept God's forgiveness and get back to the life he's given you to live. That's it, pure and simple.

A third danger zone is the area of justification. In the same way that we can be too harsh on ourselves, we can take advantage of God's grace and go too easy on ourselves. We all have habits and thought patterns and attitudes that we need to rid ourselves of; to deny that is to deny our

Test all things; hold fast what is good.

—1 THESSALONIANS 5:21 NKJV

humanity. But when we rationalize our faults time and time again, we make no discernible progress in what should be the overriding goal of our lives—to be conformed to the image of Christ.

> *Without apology and without defense we ask to see what*
> *is truly in us. It is for our own sake that we ask these things.*
> *It is for our good, for our healing, for our happiness.*
>
> —RICHARD FOSTER, *PRAYER: FINDING THE HEART'S TRUE HOME*

Chapter 25

The Christian Year

I need to start with a confession: as a Christian, I can be as arrogant as the worst of the lot. As with a young couple who believe their experience of love is like no other in history, we in the Jesus People Movement used to believe that no one in history, save the apostles, had as close a relationship with Jesus as we Jesus Freaks had. I later applied that thinking to all of evangelicalism. The expression of faith that I was connected with at any given time was the only one that actually had it together.

My Catholic friends in particular baffled me. Right after Thanksgiving a wreath with four candles would appear on their dining room tables. I didn't want to say anything, but it sure was obvious that one of the candles was a different color from the others, in every house I visited. I was fairly sure none of my Catholic friends was color blind, so I figured Catholics must be especially frugal and saw the Christmas season as an opportunity to use up all their mismatched candles.

Over the years I came to realize that these families followed some kind of ritual that involved lighting the candles one by one on certain days leading up to Christmas Day. But they always lit the three matching candles first. If it had been me, I would have lit that odd-colored candle first, the one that threw off the chromatic symmetry, and let it burn down quickly so there would at least be three matching candles. This ritual served to fuel my suspicion that Catholics believed that this endless lighting of candles, in church and at home, would somehow save them.

And Lent! That was just an invention of the Catholic Church designed to compress guilt into a six-week period so people would give more money to the church in order to be saved. Oh, those Catholics! I sure had them figured out. All those meaningless rituals! If only they would listen to me. The billions of Catholics in the world would surely fall to their knees, renounce their empty religiosity, and ask Jesus into their hearts. Then they would know what faith was all about!

God dealt with my attitude with what I recognize now as delightful irony. He made sure my life work would involve learning about and

---

Through Christian-year spirituality we are enabled to experience the biblical mandate of conforming to Christ. The Christian year orders our formation with Christ incarnate in his ministry, death, burial, resurrection, and coming again through Advent, Christmas, Epiphany, Lent, Holy Week, Easter, and Pentecost. . . . We are spiritually formed by recalling and entering in to his great saving events.

—ROBERT E. WEBBER

researching all religious beliefs, practices, symbols, traditions, rituals, and lifestyles, much of which served to underscore the shallowness and narrowness of my own expression of faith. Trust me—the education process was painful. Yes, there were abuses in the Catholic Church, and yes, there were Catholics who simply went through the motions of their faith tradition, but all that meant was that they were no different from any other Christian group—or any other non-Christian group, for that matter.

Still, I couldn't understand the emphasis that Catholics and liturgical Protestants—Episcopalians, Methodists, Lutherans, and Presbyterians—placed on what they called the church year. That is, until I became involved in a liturgical prayer center just after Christmas one year. Over those first few weeks, the reality of the Christian year began to unfold. Not that I understood it, mind you; I simply began to recognize that there was a rhythm to the weeks and months that existed quite apart from the calendar hanging on my wall. By the time Lent arrived, I knew I wanted to move to the rhythm that seemed to come so naturally to others in the church.

That rhythm has its roots in ancient tradition—Jewish tradition, in fact. The Israelites lived by the rhythm of the seasons, as did all agricultural societies, but their seasons were also tied in to the many religious feasts and festivals and holy days that served as anchors for their faith throughout the year. Maybe you've noticed in the Bible how often God told the Israelites to "remember" their history and, even more so, the history of their relationship with God. The Israelites had a profound understanding of what it meant to remember those milestones in their past; each time they observed a holy

Instead, as you share in the sufferings of the Messiah rejoice, so that
you may also rejoice with great joy at the revelation of His glory.

—1 PETER 4:13 HCSB

day, they experienced it as if it were actually happening in present time. You can readily see that in the modern-day Jewish observance of Passover. It's more than a memorial; it's a lived experience. The Jewish liturgical year became its own lived experience.

Jews who became followers of Christ kept this tradition alive, choosing instead to anchor their year with days that were significant to them, such as Jesus' resurrection day, which later became known as Easter, and Pentecost. And in terms of lived experience in the Christian church, communion is considered by many to be much more than an occasional reminder of the Last Supper; it's a deeply significant ritual that reflects the Hebrew understanding of "remember," one that strengthens and energizes their faith.

At any rate, by the fourth century, Christians had developed a fairly substantial liturgical year. In the journal she kept during her pilgrimage to Palestine in the fourth century, Egeria offers an extensive description of the liturgy that the church in Jerusalem used on special days, like the Feast of the Epiphany and Pentecost, and also during Lent. Those who think Lent is a purely Roman Catholic invention, as I once did, have only to leaf through (or scroll through, thanks to the Internet) Egeria's journal to realize that the observance of Lent was well under way, at least in Jerusalem, in the first few centuries after Christ.

But back to our modern liturgical calendar, which began to take shape in the medieval church. The liturgical year, in ancient times as well as today, serves as a reminder of the basics of our faith, through symbols

Liturgy is rehearsal of the whole story of Jesus' ministry, passion, death, resurrection; liturgy is doing something together in the light of the gospel.

—JOHN J. VINCENT

used in decorating the church building for each season or special day, the different colors and styles of vestments worn by the clergy, and the specific Bible passages, hymns, and sermon topics that are chosen with regard to the focus of the season. Think of Christmas in the evangelical church—how for weeks everything from the way the church looks to the songs we sing is centered on that one day of celebration. In liturgical churches, it's that way throughout the year, to a lesser degree overall, of course, but also to varying degrees among denominations and from one parish to another.

You can imagine how crucial all this symbolism was in communicating the gospel to an illiterate society. To walk into a church building was to become immersed in the great truths of Christianity, especially if the building was a cathedral—which I probably shouldn't even mention because that means running the risk of getting sidetracked onto another topic entirely, which of course is the architectural magnificence and spiritual symbolism of those truly awesome structures that sometimes represented hundreds of years of work and always represented tremendous personal sacrifice and which I could write a whole book about and may actually do someday.

To be involved in many liturgical churches today is to likewise become immersed in the rhythm of the faith, starting with the first day of Advent, which is always the fourth Sunday before Christmas—hence, the four candles in the Advent wreath. (I later learned that the one odd-colored candle was intentional, since it symbolizes the joy that Advent is nearly over and Christmas is at hand. Imagine my chagrin.) This is a time of solemn anticipation; a kind of holy hush descends on the church as we await the

The time is fulfilled, and the kingdom of God has come near.

—MARK 1:15 HCSB

coming of the newborn King. It's also a time of repentance as we prepare our hearts to receive the Savior. The days grow shorter and darker, but we are at an advantage: we know the Light of the World is about to be born.

Let me tell you—my first Advent season in a liturgical church was like no other I had ever experienced. It was as Christ-centered as pre-Christmas in America can possibly be. Who knew? Part of the irony of that question stems from the profound reverence toward God that the liturgical year inspires.

Back in the 1970s I visited an inner-city denominational church in the Northeast one Sunday morning; it was one of those churches and congregations that had seen better, and I hope livelier, days in the nineteenth century. The sanctuary was utterly cavernous, and yet there were fewer than fifty people at this, the main Sunday worship service. There was complete silence as we walked in and nearly complete silence thereafter. I felt like jumping out of my skin. This was a dead church for certain; unfortunately, I mentally and unwittingly set this one church up as a standard by which to judge all mainline denominational churches for years afterwards.

So when I entered a liturgical church in the 1990s—the first time I had dared to give a mainline church another try—and encountered the same silence, I interpreted it as a sign that this, too, was a dead church.

In the fullness of time, God invades our history, assumes our flesh, heals, teaches, and eats with sinners. . . . The centrality of time in Christianity is reflected in Christian worship. This worship, like the rest of life, is structured on recurring rhythms of the day, the week, and the year. . . . How we structure time enables us to commemorate and re-experience those very acts on which salvation is grounded.

—HOYT L. HICKMAN, *THE NEW HANDBOOK OF THE CHRISTIAN YEAR*

WHAT ALL THOSE COLORS MEAN

If the idea of following the liturgical year sounds appealing to you, you may be interested in the symbolism behind the colors used in liturgical churches at different times of the year. Some people actually coordinate their clothing with the current color, especially on special Sundays and other observances. Believe it or not, this custom has nothing to do with fashion and everything to do with being symbolically clothed in the truth of Christ that the season represents. That's all well and good if you have a perfect, polychromatic skin tone, but during the longest season of the Christian year—the "green" season—I'm afraid I'd scare off half the congregation. Green and I should never coexist outside an ICU room.

Pay attention now, because color significance gets confusing since denominations don't always use the same colors at the same time:

Green symbolizes hope and is closely tied to the idea of new life associated with the spring harvest. It's used on certain feast days, the ordinary time between Epiphany and Lent, and throughout ordinary time between Pentecost and Advent.

White represents purity, of course. White is the color of choice for Christmas and Easter, and again, certain feast days, though gold is sometimes used instead.

Many have undertaken to compile a narrative about the events that have been fulfilled among us, just as the original eyewitnesses and servants of the word handed them down to us. It also seemed good to me, since I have carefully investigated everything from the very first, to write to you in orderly sequence, most honorable Theophilus, so that you may know the certainty of the things about which you have been instructed.

—LUKE 1:1–4 HCSB

Black, as you might suspect, is used on somber occasions to represent death and sin. It's used during Advent to symbolize the darkness the world was in before Jesus, the Light of the world, was born. Black is also worn during Lent as a solemn reminder of the suffering and death of Jesus that lies ahead. Technically, no color is used during Lent and the Great Triduum; but then again, black is actually the absence of color, so it fits.

Purple is also a no-brainer—or so I thought. It's the color of royalty and represents Jesus as the King of kings—right? No. It's actually the color of mourning—specifically, mourning over our sins. It's used on Sundays during Advent and Lent and during some days of Holy Week. And all that time I figured we were celebrating the coming or the resurrection of the King. (In some traditions, blue replaces purple during Advent.)

Red is associated with blood and fire and is a natural for Pentecost, when tongues of fire descended on the Christians assembled in Jerusalem following the Crucifixion. It's also used on certain feast days or other special days.

Not so. In that church I soon recognized that silence as a sign of reverence and not death or empty religiosity. I'm not saying this is true in all liturgical churches, and I'm not saying that evangelicals should do away with socializing before the service begins; there have been times when I needed the kind of free and easy human contact that we often experience in non-liturgical churches. What I'm saying is that the observance of the liturgical year seems to inspire a deep reverence for God, and that reverence is tangible.

Back to Advent, which of course precedes Christmas. I had never realized that many Christians avoid singing carols until Christmas Day, which is why the choral presentations and congregational singing are so important at midnight services and Christmas Eve vigils in many churches. Again, an illiterate society—or even a literate society steeped in Christian symbolism—would have understood this instinctively. Me, I had to learn it on my own.

With Christmas, light comes into the world through our Savior, Jesus Christ, and the emphasis shifts from the anticipated hope of Advent to the fulfilled hope of Christmas—and to an emphasis on the Incarnation, a word we don't hear often enough in non-liturgical churches. The Incarnation becomes the focus of the readings, the songs, and the sermons during the Christmas season, which extends right through until the eve of the Feast of the Epiphany on January 6, the Twelfth Night of Christmas. Epiphany marks the manifestation of Jesus as the Son of God through the visit of the Magi.

Next follows a three-week period of "ordinary" time (more about that later) known as the *septuagesima,* when the attention of the church is directed toward the manifestation of Jesus in our personal lives. That period ends with the penitential season of Lent, which brings me back to my first exposure to the rhythm of the liturgical year.

Lent is followed by Holy Week, which is one of the church year traditions that evangelicals have wisely held on to. Palm Sunday, Maundy Thursday, and Good Friday are all familiar to us, with their rituals steeped in biblical tradition. Lesser known are the liturgical rituals of the Great Triduum—the three days from Maundy Thursday to Holy Saturday and the Great Easter Vigil of Saturday night. For many believers around the world, these three days are set aside for prayer, fasting, and solemn reflection. Many people stop their normal routines during the Great Triduum, taking vacation days then so they can devote their time and attention to God.

In churches that celebrate the Great Triduum, everything changes. There's no instrumental music during the Triduum. At the end of the

Maundy Thursday service, the communion table and the altar are stripped of all that they once held, a reminder that Jesus was stripped of his garments before the crucifixion. All decoration and ornamentation are removed from the church as the congregation sits in silence and near-darkness. The symbolism is unmistakable. The quiet, somber mood continues through Good Friday and the Great Easter Vigil of Holy Saturday, a time when some Christians stay up all night, often at the church, as a way of entering into the suffering of Jesus. Because they have likely been fasting as well, the all-night vigil is particularly difficult and painful. This is an intensely personal experience. People become so immersed in the events of those three days that there are lots of tissue boxes spread throughout the sanctuary. For the first time in my life as a Christian, I needed one or two of those boxes all to myself the first time I truly experienced the Great Triduum.

The sunrise services of Easter morning—long a tradition in evangelical churches—continue a tradition started by the ancients in the first century. They, however, often held sunrise services, including those on every day throughout Lent and every Sunday throughout the year. Like Christmas, Easter is a day of joyful celebration, made all the more meaningful by the penitential seasons that precede each of those major holy days. And just as the Christmas season does not end on Christmas Day, the Easter season does not end on Easter Sunday. It lasts for fifty joyous and alleluia-saturated days that focus on resurrection life. Easter ends with Pentecost, which used to be known as Whitsunday, which sounds oh-so-British and much classier. We all know what happened at Pentecost, right? The Holy Spirit descended on the church, and the world was changed for all time.

Ironically, though, the season after Pentecost in May and extending all the way through Advent in November is known as "ordinary" time. You'd think after Pentecost nothing would be considered ordinary. But of course, "ordinary" in the context of the church year takes on a special meaning. The extraordinary events that we celebrate between Advent and Pentecost have transformed us; now it's time for us to become true disciples of Christ. Ordinary time gives us the opportunity to catch our breath, settle into the Sunday-to-Sunday routine, and allow God to change us into the people he wants us to be.

That's it. That's the liturgical year in a sweeping overview. I've omitted much out of necessity—some of the great feast days and other observances that I have come to love. We all experience different kinds of "years"—the calendar year, which is universal, but also other ways of marking off time, such as the school year or the fiscal year or the dreaded political year. But none has so thoroughly seeped into my spirit as the liturgical year has.

Chapter 26

Contemporary Asceticism

The way of the ascetic is a way of renunciation and self-discipline—in other words, a way that runs counter to our nature. We don't like giving up our creature comforts, and we don't like the hard work it takes to bring our desires under control and replace them with an active hungering and thirsting for the things of God. That's especially true when we equate all that with the word *asceticism,* which many people—if not most people—associate with an attempt to earn our salvation through extreme self-denial, self-injury, and a host of other questionable practices.

The Greek word on which we base the English word *asceticism* is *askesis,* which means training or exercise. Early ascetics pursued the life they did because they believed they were called to undergo training in the rigors of the Christian life in order to better know and serve God. Theirs

A MODERN-DAY ASCETIC

Singer and songwriter Rich Mullins shocked all but those who knew him when he left the Nashville recording industry to teach music to children on a Navajo reservation, accepting a salary equivalent to what his teaching colleagues made. That came as no surprise, though, to friends, family, and industry insiders who saw in Rich a man who wanted nothing but to serve Christ and live as Christ lived. He took a vow of poverty and even started a religious "order," the Kid Brothers of St. Frank, out of his desire to emulate the life of Francis of Assisi. The proceeds from his concerts and his record sales went straight to his church and from there to several charities, including Compassion International and Compassion USA. Rich also served as a missionary with Compassion. He never married. He was killed in a car crash in 1997 at the age of forty-one.

was a strict and at times severe lifestyle focused on prayer, contemplation, solitude, hard work, and renouncing evil and comfort. And they believed Jesus meant it when he told his followers to be perfect (see Matt. 5:48).

Though many ascetics lived emotionally, mentally, and physically healthy lives (John the Baptist immediately comes to mind), others allowed excesses to take over. It wasn't enough to live on bread and water; some made a test out of seeing just how little they could live on. That was more than a bit self-defeating, because you can't exactly figure out how little

Therefore you are to be perfect, as your heavenly Father is perfect.
—MATTHEW 5:48 NASB

you can live on until you reach the point of not living on that next lesser amount in other words, until you've died. This was the kind of practice that gave asceticism a bad name. "Such regulations," wrote Paul, "indeed have an appearance of wisdom, with their self-imposed worship, their false humility and their harsh treatment of the body, but they lack any value in restraining sensual indulgence" (Col. 2:23 NIV).

What the extremists in the ascetic movement failed to grasp, I think, was a full understanding of self-discipline. It's not enough to discipline ourselves to live a life of renunciation and self-denial; we need to discipline ourselves to live a life of *responsible* renunciation and self-denial—in other words, to know when enough is enough. Our self-control is working properly when it enables us to stop eating so much; it is not working properly when it drives us to stop eating altogether. It is also working properly when we resist temptation; it is not working properly when we beat ourselves silly because we had a lustful thought. One of the hallmarks of godly asceticism is humility—not self-humiliation.

Asceticism may sound a lot like a lifestyle built on a "works righteousness"—the belief that by following all these practices, the ascetic would find favor with God and thus attain salvation. Certainly some ascetics believed that and to this day continue in that deception. Others were simply blind to the fact that what they were doing was trying to earn their salvation. But it's clear from the writings of some of the best-known ascetics that they believed that they were called to an ascetic life and to fail to live it would be a failure to obey Christ. Some went so far as to say that

> *However great your zeal and many the efforts of your asceticism,*
> *they are all in vain and without useful result*
> *unless they attain to love in a broken spirit.*
>
> —SYMEON THE NEW THEOLOGIAN

all Christians have been called to a life of asceticism, that renunciation and self-discipline are the factors that distinguish a Christian lifestyle from a worldly one.

So early ascetics renounced worldly living and set themselves apart by living in a distinctly different way. But what are some of the things a contemporary ascetic may be called to renounce? Here are a few:

- Consumerism: the desire to acquire and possess not only more things but bigger (or smaller) and better and cooler and more cutting-edge things.

- Entertainment: not just in the form of television and movies, which is what we normally think of, but any leisure activity that distracts from the ascetic's pursuit of God or drains finances and resources that could be used more wisely.

- Sex and marriage: ascetics are not always called to a celibate life, though some are. They know that they will never marry, and they know that means they will never have sex (or never have it again). Jesus spoke without judgment of people who "renounced marriage because of the kingdom of heaven" (Matt. 19:12 NIV).

- Money: ascetics may be called to live well below the poverty level, though their incomes may be significantly higher. Any excess is to be given to the poor.

- Unnecessary talk: ascetics take Proverbs 21:23 literally: "He who guards his mouth and tongue guards his soul from troubles" (NASB).

> *Jesus said to him, "If you wish to be complete, go and sell your possessions and give to the poor, and you shall have treasure in heaven; and come, follow Me."*
>
> —MATTHEW 19:21 NASB

- Anything that fosters selfishness: a true ascetic willingly and joyfully gives up anything, even something as intangible as a special privilege, that causes her to feel any degree of selfishness.

When you look at the list above and remove the twenty-first century trappings, what you see has got to be unsettling to Christians today, because what you see is the church as it was described in Acts, along with Jesus' teachings and the teachings in the New Testament epistles. There's at least a fair-to-middling chance that those who say all Christians are called to an ascetic life are actually right.

Evangelical author and professor Dallas Willard defines the disciplines of abstinence, or the contemporary living-out of asceticism, as silence, solitude, fasting, frugality, chastity, sacrifice, and secrecy (about your good deeds and qualities). Other private disciplines include prayer and study. Unlike the desert dwellers, Willard places equal importance on relational disciplines, such as celebration, service, and fellowship, among others. These disciplines, he believes, are not only possible in twenty-first century America but also essential for anyone wishing to live an authentic Christian life. I really like his take on sensible asceticism; as he puts it, asceticism is "just good sense about life and ultimately, about spiritual life."

Christian asceticism is not spiritual boot camp, but neither is it effortless. Learning when and how, to what, and to whom to give our yes or our no is a lifelong project.

—M. Shawn Copeland

Chapter 27

Fasting

As a woman who has struggled with blood-sugar disorders her entire life, I'm hardly in a position to be spouting off about fasting. I cannot fast the way I once did now that I've been diagnosed with diabetes. The best I can do is admit that this is one of the few spiritual practices that I can't participate in, but I can encourage you to give it a try based on my prior experience.

Fortunately, this is also a spiritual practice that is familiar to evangelicals, though I wonder how many have actually given it a try. I don't remember it being emphasized or practiced in the nondenominational evangelical church I attended, but I have since discovered that charismatics take fasting seriously. They seem to fast more often and for more reasons than other groups.

For the most part I'd fast one meal or, occasionally, an entire day each week. That was as much as I felt I could or should fast, given my physical limitations. For several years in the 1970s, I was on a major health-food kick and felt that my blood sugar was under control enough that I could attempt a longer fast. At the time, I was going through one of those situations euphemistically called a "rough patch," and I felt as if God was calling me to several days of fasting to seek clarity regarding my own contribution to the problem at hand.

Despite all I'd read about fasting and all my friends had told me about their experiences with fasting, I was not prepared for either the physical ramifications or the spiritual impact it had on my life. The first three days of my water-only fast were decidedly unpleasant. The headaches, the hunger pains that were no longer mere pangs, the fuzzy thinking and light-headedness—it's a wonder I managed not only to get to work each day but to also retain my job in the process. As a reporter at a busy daily newspaper, I was not in any position to kick back and take it easy for those first three days. More than once I was tempted to quit. Fasting, that is, not my job.

But then, almost as if by an act of God, after seventy-two hours every disagreeable symptom disappeared. Just like that, the pain, the discomfort, the mental fog all vanished. For the next three days, I felt better than I had felt before I began the fast. My energy level, which had sunk to an abysmally low point over the first three days, shot right back up and beyond

---

Widows and virgins are to fast often and pray for the Church.
Priests as well as laity are to fast as they wish. The bishop can fast
only when the entire people fasts, for it may be that someone wants to
make an offering and the bishop cannot refuse it.

—HIPPOLYTUS, *APOSTOLIC TRADITION,* AD 315

WHY FAST?

The Renovaré Spiritual Formation Bible defines fasting as "the voluntary abstention from a normal function—most often eating—for the sake of intense spiritual activity." The goal is to combine fasting with other spiritual practices, such as prayer and meditation, in order to grow closer to God. The reasons why fasting is so beneficial to our spiritual lives are many. Here are a few:

- When we abstain from food, we free our minds from having to think about an ordinary activity like eating. We also free up the time we would normally spend preparing a meal, eating the meal, and cleaning up afterwards. It's amazing how much time all that takes over the course of a day. And when you factor in the time we spend just *thinking* about food, well, the whole day's pretty well shot.
- Fasting reveals a great deal about ourselves: what our priorities are, how cranky we can be at times, how often we turn to

what it had been before. My thinking was crystal clear. My writing felt effortless. And those were just the physical results; I haven't even gotten to the good part yet.

How many different ways can you describe how special your time with God has been? I suppose that if I took the time, I could come up with dozens of images that would give you an idea of what it was like to have an encounter with God under the conditions of that fast. What really matters,

When I heard these words, I sat down and wept. I mourned for a number of days, fasting and praying before the God of heaven.

—NEHEMIAH 1:4 HCSB

food for comfort and a release from anxiety, how much time and food we waste.

- Depriving our bodies of the food we've come to depend on causes us to turn to God as the One we can always depend on.

- Self-denial, when practiced for the right reasons, always leads to a greater degree of self-control.

- Whenever we purposely suffer, we become better equipped to handle hardships in the future, and we become more sensitive to those around us who are suffering.

- Developing the habit of fasting adds to our growing awareness of the value of spiritual exercises and the impact they can have on our relationship with God.

- Fasting sharpens our senses and our sensitivity to the Holy Spirit, which makes it an invaluable activity when you're seeking clarity on an important matter.

Then the king went to his palace and spent the night fasting. No diversions were brought to him, and he could not sleep.

—DANIEL 6:18 HCSB

Jesus hath many lovers of his heavenly kingdom, but few bearers of his Cross. He hath many seekers of comfort, but few of tribulation. He findeth many companions of his table, but few of his fasting. All desire to rejoice with him, few are willing to undergo anything for his sake. . . . If Jesus hide himself and withdraw a little while, they fall either into complaining or into too great dejection of mind.

—THOMAS À KEMPIS, *THE IMITATION OF CHRIST*

though, was the end result, and I wasn't at the end yet. I had questions, lots of questions. How would I know when to end the fast? Had the fast already accomplished what I had hoped it would? Was I continuing the fast for all the wrong reasons?

I had started the fast on a Monday morning, and by Saturday night I had the answers to those questions. The time had come to end the fast. The fast had accomplished what I hoped it would, but deep down I knew that didn't mean the situation would be resolved the way I wanted it to be; time eventually confirmed that my gut feeling about that was accurate. To have continued the fast beyond that point would have been an act of pride—"Let me see how long I can go without food! I'll bet I can fast longer than anyone else I know!" I had not felt the slightest degree of hunger for three days. I broke the fast with a glass of orange juice mixed with protein powder and went to bed, fully at peace with God and with what had once been an ugly, turmoil-filled situation.

According to Mary Margaret Funk, the fast I undertook is known as a water-purification fast because I abstained from food entirely—which is what we normally think of when we hear the word *fast*. Funk views fasting from a different perspective, one she describes as "the middle way." This type of fasting calls for you to eat just enough of what is offered or available to you, at appointed times for each meal. Both overeating and undereating,

---

Go and assemble all the Jews who can be found
in Susa and fast for me. Don't eat or drink
for three days, night and day. I and my
female servants will also fast in the same way.
After that, I will go to the king even
if it is against the law. If I perish, I perish.

—ESTHER 4:16 HCSB

she points out, make us sluggish, while eating the correct amount keeps us alert and well-nourished.

Regardless of what the different kinds of fasts are called and what they entail, Funk believes the biblical approach to eating requires that we not allow food to take center stage, which is going to be a tough sell in our society. Even when we depart from fasting—say, when we're entertaining guests or participating in a celebration—the focus should be on the people and the cause for the occasion rather than on the food, she maintains. She gets no argument from me, but try convincing someone who just spent three days preparing the perfect meal for some special event.

Throughout history and in different cultures, the rules and customs regarding fasting have always varied. The Jews have generally fasted as a sign of mourning or repentance, or in observance of a religious holiday. They fast for twenty-five hours on certain holidays, from sundown one day to an hour after sundown the next day. On other holidays, they follow a modified fast, from sunrise to sunset. Daniel fasted on vegetables and water; Jesus went without food entirely for forty days. Our desert friends imitated Christ in this regard, undergoing extensive fasts and living on next to nothing at other times. Antony, whom we know well by now, lived on little but bread and water for years at a time. On rare occasions, people underwent a

The attitude of Jesus to the Jewish law was singularly free and unembarrassed. . . . Such freehanded dealing meant that the whole notion of morality as a code of rules, with sanctions of rewards and punishments, was abandoned. But the average Christian was slow to see this implication. For instance, Jesus had taken fasting out of the class of meritorious acts, and given it a place only as the fitting and spontaneous expression of certain spiritual states.

—C. HAROLD DODD

total fast, abstaining from food and water for three days—the longest the human body can go without water. That's what Esther asked the Jewish people to do before she approached the king on behalf of her people.

The *Didache* laid down the law for the early church: "Do not let your fasts be with the hypocrites. They fast on Monday and Thursday, but you shall fast on Wednesday and Friday." If you know your New Testament, you know who the "hypocrites" were—the Pharisees, who regularly fasted on Mondays and Thursdays. The writer of the *Didache* wanted to be sure no one associated this new Christian sect with the Pharisees and, therefore, set aside two different days, Wednesday and Friday, as fast days for Christians.

Some monastic orders, like the Benedictines, serve only one small meal per day. Other orders go the three-meal-a-day route, but the quantity of their food intake varies wildly. One monastery I visited had a virtual all-you-can-eat buffet at every meal for the monks and visitors alike; another provided fairly substantial meals that were often a hodge-podge of leftovers, which meant they were making good use of the contributions of food and money they received. A third offered truly healthful, delicious meals in moderate amounts that still managed to fill me up.

Today, practicing Christians sometimes abstain from eating certain foods, particularly "trigger" foods that can lead to overeating. Dieters do this to lose weight, of course, but when it's done as a spiritual practice, the purpose is to develop self-control and avoid gluttony. There's also a trend

> *Yet when they were sick,*
> *my clothing was sackcloth;*
> *I humbled myself with fasting,*
> *and my prayer was genuine.*
>
> —PSALM 35:13 HCSB

today, both within and outside of Christian circles, to reduce our food intake to the amount that a poor person in a developing nation might eat on an average day, as a way of sharing in the suffering of others.

I guess I've reached the point where I have to do what I really, really don't want to do. I need to advise you to never begin a fast without your doctor's approval, or if you have any physical problems that may be complicated by fasting, or if you're pregnant, or if you're a child—in which case you need to beg your parents to buy you some age-appropriate reading material.

Some of you can sustain life with less food than others can, and therefore I desire that he who needs more nourishment shall not be obliged to equal others, but that every one shall give his body what it needs for being an efficient servant of the soul. For as we are obliged to be on our guard against superfluous food which injures body and soul alike, thus we must be on the watch against immoderate fasting, and this the more, because the Lord wants conversion and not victims.

—Francis of Assisi

Chapter 28

Saying a Blessing

When we evangelicals speak of saying a blessing, we are most likely referring to the act of "saying grace"—blessing the meal at hand. One of the things I've come to understand is that our desire to practice certain rituals is often at the mercy of the dynamics of a particular household. In some homes, saying grace feels hollow and empty no matter how significant it may be to one member of the household—especially when the atmosphere of the home is consistently charged with tension. I can't begin to count the number of times I've been in a home where someone contentious says grace only because he's been forced to by his wife or by the teachings of his church or by his own need to appear spiritual and assert his role as the spiritual head of the household. Let me be clear—I'm not judging these men or anyone else in that kind of position. On the contrary,

I empathize with them in some cases. I'm just saying that reciting grace over meals has felt insincere often enough that I've sometimes pulled way back from the practice. Now I just say a silent prayer.

However, if I could figure out a way to make saying grace a meaningful ritual again, I'd do it in a heartbeat, or so I'd like to think. Maybe one way would be to incorporate the Jewish practice of saying prayers not just before meals but afterwards, as well, which actually has a biblical precedent: "When you have eaten and are full, then you shall bless the LORD your God for the good land which He has given you" (Deut. 8:10 NKJV). Now there's an idea—asking God to bless the meal before we partake of it, and then asking him to bless our digestive tracts afterwards. But that's not the intent. While the prayer before meals is short and to the point, the postprandial prayer covers a lot of territory, thanking God for filling the body and the universe with food and goodness.

Blessing the meal and the hands that prepared it is the most common form of blessing in Christian homes, other than the "bless you" or "bless your heart" that peppers our conversation at times. It doesn't occur to us to pronounce a blessing over every little thing in our lives. But one culture, the Celts, did, and another, the Jews, still do. With the revival of interest in Celtic spirituality over the past decade, the practice of blessing the mundane is returning, or so it would seem if the number of related books being published is any indication.

One of the reasons why Celtic Christianity appeals to the spiritual sensibilities of some Christians is that it resonates with what we know of

> *The Lord be with you always, and be you with him*
> *always and in every place.*
>
> —CLARE OF ASSISI

the early church and what we hunger for in the contemporary church. In the Celts we find a "whole person" spirituality, one that fully integrates the entire person—body, mind, and spirit—and the entire Christian community, with no denominational distinctions. But how were the Celts able to manage that? How did they stay out of the fray that resulted in the divided church that we have today? Celtic scholar Esther de Waal says we can attribute that in part to the simple matter of geography; the Celtic Christians flourished spiritually because they lived and worshiped in the more remote areas of the British Isles, outside the reach of ecclesiastical authority and the political infighting in the Western Church.

Much of what we know about the Celtic habit of blessing everyone and everything we owe to the research of a man named Alexander Carmichael, who in the late nineteenth century traveled throughout the areas inhabited by the ancient Celts and discovered Christians who routinely used specific blessings that had been handed down through the centuries.

These weren't simple one-liners, though those existed as well; these were multiversed songs or chants that family and friends would assemble to sing as a visitor resumed his travels or an older child left home—or a new child was born. Others were more personal and private. One of my favorites is a blessing the women would say as they lit the fire in the hearth each morning, blessing not only the fire for the warmth it provided but also the fire that they asked God to kindle and keep alive in their hearts.

The Celts blessed every activity in their lives, from major milestones like getting married to routine work like making the bed and churning the

Being reviled, we bless; being persecuted, we endure it.

—1 CORINTHIANS 4:12B NKJV

butter and plowing the field. As writer Ray Simpson notes, the operative phrase is "in their lives." The Celts understood that there needed to be a personal connection with the item or the activity or a personal relationship with the person they were blessing. They took their cue from the Old Testament, where every instance of blessing involved a relationship on some level. "To go around blessing people or objects in a perfunctory way is magic; it is not of God," writes Simpson.

To give you an idea of what these blessings were like, here is one verse of a blessing that was said when milking a cow, from de Waal's *The Celtic Way of Prayer*:

> Bless, O God, my little cow,
> Bless, O God, my desire;
> Bless Thou my partnership
> And the milking of my hands, O God.

Since not many of us milk cows these days, contemporary Celtic blessings have been developed for our computers (may they never crash!) and the like. Some of these blessings do lose a lot in the translation, though; the ancient Celtic blessings were beautiful, even those that applied to unbeautiful things like fertilizer. If modern language works for you, then go for it. I'm inclined either to write my own blessings or use some from Simpson's compilation, *Celtic Blessings: Prayers for Everyday Life,* many of which retain the beauty of the Celtic way of expressing prayer.

In thy journeys to and fro God direct thee;
In thy happiness and pleasure God bless thee;
In care, anxiety or trouble God sustain thee;
In peril and in danger God protect thee.

—TIMOTHY OLUFOSOYE

Like the Celts, the Jews have or have had a blessing for pretty much everything in life—so much so that Judaism has been called the "way of blessing." (There's even an alleged blessing to be pronounced after going to the bathroom.) Even if your familiarity with the Hebrew Scriptures (our Old Testament) is sketchy, you probably recall some of the instances of blessing that you've read about; it's easy to see from the Scriptures how the Jewish faith came to be so closely associated with the concept of blessing.

When Rebekah left home to become Isaac's wife, her family said this blessing over her: "Our sister, may you become the mother of thousands of ten thousands; and may your descendants possess the gates of those who hate them" (Gen. 24:60 NKJV). The Hebrews had no problem pronouncing such an honest blessing as that one. Years later, when it was Isaac's turn to bless his sons, he did so with equal honesty as he pronounced these words over Jacob:

> Therefore may God give you
> Of the dew of heaven,
> Of the fatness of the earth,
> And plenty of grain and wine.
> Let peoples serve you,
> And nations bow down to you.
> Be master over your brethren,
> And let your mother's sons bow down to you.
> Cursed be everyone who curses you,

Then David returned to bless his household.

—2 SAMUEL 6:20A NKJV

And blessed be those who bless you!

(Gen. 27:28–29 NKJV)

When the time came for Jacob to die, he gathered his twelve sons together, "blessing each one with his own special farewell blessing" (Gen. 49:28 MSG). The words he spoke, recorded in Genesis 49, became prophetic words for the twelve tribes of Israel that his sons represented. As Ray Simpson points out, the act of blessing is invaluable when it is linked with "knowledge, wisdom, or the gift of 'seeing,'" such as that which was evident in Jacob's blessing.

Then there's this admonition against blessing others, found in Proverbs 27:14: "He who blesses his friend with a loud voice, rising early in the morning, it will be counted a curse to him" (NKJV). Thankfully, when Jesus came along, bringing the new covenant with him, he made a point of advising his followers to cease and desist from all that cursing.

Modern-day Jews have eliminated all that cursing, as well. Aside from the blessings attached to rituals, like those related to the Sabbath or studying the Torah (the first five books of the Bible), observant Jews are also likely to say a blessing when they are struck by something especially powerful or beautiful in nature, when they receive good news or bad news, and when something new or unusual occurs. Most of all, they routinely pronounce blessings over rites of passage in the family—birth, graduation, engagement, marriage, and death.

The Celtic world . . . remains totally unique, earthy, and mysterious, knowing darkness and pain but equally rejoicing in light, full of poetry and song and celebration, showing me the depths of penitence and the heights of praise, touching me in the secret hidden parts of my own self and yet connecting me with others.

—ESTHER DE WAAL, *THE CELTIC WAY OF PRAYER*

Reviving the ancient practice of blessing and incorporating it into our lives is easier than you may think. It's also one of those traditions that you probably should ease into when practicing it around others. In private, you can get away with blessing the remote control, I suppose, but when you start blessing ordinary items within earshot of others, you're on shaky ground.

For years I've integrated blessing into my life by signing cards, letters, and an occasional e-mail with what I call "may" blessings—benedictions like "May the Lord richly bless you" or "May you be wrapped in God's love." When you start to think in terms of "may" blessings, the practice of blessing others quickly becomes a habit, and you discover that you're less likely to have to struggle to find the right words to express your thoughts. That's particularly helpful when you're sending your condolences to someone who is grieving. We often find ourselves at a loss for words, which is actually a blessing in itself when we're in the presence of the mourner; in that case, the less we say the better. But when we need to send our condolences in writing, we're inclined to get stuck. Giving thought to what you would like to see God do in that person's life and then phrasing it in a "may" statement ("May God comfort you and your children and provide for your every need at this time") can often get you unstuck.

Let me leave you with this blessing: May God help you discern which traditions of the ancients will draw you closer to him, and may you delight in them even as you delight in him.

Then Toi sent Joram his son to King David,
to greet him and bless him.

—2 SAMUEL 8:10A NKJV

Selected and Annotated Bibliography

Barry, William A., and William J. Connolly. *The Practice of Spiritual Direction.* New York: Seabury Press, 1982.

Bettenson, Henry, and Chris Maunder, eds. *Documents of the Christian Church.* 3rd ed. Oxford: Oxford University Press, 1999.

Borst, James. *Contemplative Prayer: A Guide for Today's Catholic.* Liguori, MO: Liguori Publications, 1979.

The Cloud of Unknowing. Available online at www.ccel.org (Christian Classics Ethereal Library, a great site where you can download Christian documents and books in the public domain). Enter "Cloud of Unknowing" in the Search box.

Cornwall, Judson. *Praying the Scriptures: Communicating with God in His Own Words.* Lake Mary, FL: Creation House, 1988. Excellent introduction to the subject, as well as an examination of the problems many people have with prayer.

de Waal, Esther. *The Celtic Way of Prayer.* New York: Doubleday, 1997.

Ellsberg, Robert. *All Saints: Daily Reflections on Saints, Prophets, and Witnesses for Our Time.* New York: Crossroad, 1997. More than any other book, this one has driven my curiosity and thirst for more information about some of the people whose lives have profoundly enriched our spiritual heritage.

Foster, Richard J. *Prayer: Finding the Heart's True Home*. San Francisco: HarperSanFrancisco, 1992. I am indebted to Foster for so much—an expanded awareness and deeper understanding of the spiritual disciplines, for starters—but his magnificent volume on prayer proved particularly invaluable to me for my purposes here.

Funk, Mary Margaret. *Tools Matter for Practicing the Spiritual Life*. New York: Continuum, 2001.

Geffen, Rela M. *Celebration and Renewal: Rites of Passage in Judaism*. Philadelphia: Jewish Publication Society, 1993. Great resource on Jewish rituals and traditions.

Green, Michael. *Evangelism in the Early Church*. Revised edition. Grand Rapids: Eerdmans, 2003. Scholarly but accessible. Anyone interested in the evangelistic philosophy and methods of the early Christians would do well to check out this book.

Hurtado, Larry W. *Lord Jesus Christ: Devotion to Jesus in Earliest Christianity*. Grand Rapids: Eerdmans, 2003. This highly academic work concerns itself primarily with underscoring the lordship of Jesus Christ in the early church but was also useful in confirming my research from other sources on certain rituals and the early liturgy.

Jungmann, Josef A. *The Early Liturgy to the Time of Gregory the Great*. Notre Dame, IN: University of Notre Dame Press, 1959.

Jurgens, William A. *The Faith of the Early Fathers*. Collegeville, MN: The Liturgical Press, 1970–1979. A three-volume academic series covering the writings of church fathers—including those who were later labeled as heretics—through about 750.

McGinn, Bernard. *The Presence of God: A History of Western Mysticism*. New York: Crossroad, 1994–1998. This three-volume series (*The Foundations of Mysticism, The Growth of Mysticism, The Flowering of Mysticism*) offers a wealth of information on this often misunderstood expression of faith.

Meeks, Wayne A. *The First Urban Christians: The Social World of the Apostle Paul*. New Haven: Yale University Press, 2003. I found this book in a retreat center library and had precious little time with it. But in that short time I learned about the practice of holding memorial meals in cemeteries, making those few minutes more valuable than seemed possible.

Meissner, W. W. *To the Greater Glory: A Psychological Study of Ignatian Spirituality.* Milwaukee: Marquette University Press, 1998.

Milavec, Aaron. *The Didache: Faith, Hope, & Life of the Earliest Christian Communities, 50–70 C.E.* Mahwah, NJ: Newman Press/Paulist Press, 2003. The most thorough and readable volume I've found on the *Didache*, a first-century manual for training Christian converts. It's a wonderful resource for understanding how the early church introduced converts to the ramifications of their new life in Christ.

Mitchell, Leonel L. *The Meaning of Ritual.* New York: Paulist Press, 1977. A slim but exceedingly helpful volume I chanced upon in a used-book store, reminding me never to underestimate the value of a one-dollar, bargain-bin find.

Nouwen, Henri J. M. *The Way of the Heart.* New York: Ballantine, 1981.

Simpson, Ray. *Celtic Blessings: Prayers for Everyday Life.* Chicago: Loyola, 1999.

The Way of a Pilgrim. Helen Bacovcin, trans. New York: Image, 1978.

Webber, Robert E. *Ancient–Future Time: Forming Spirituality through the Christian Year.* Grand Rapids: Baker Books, 2004. A thorough overview of the Christian year that is especially relevant to evangelicals who have never experienced the Christian year and question its value. Part of Webber's wonderful *Ancient–Future* book series.

Willard, Dallas. *The Spirit of the Disciplines.* San Francisco: HarperSanFrancisco, 1991.

About the Author

On her way to becoming an English teacher, Marcia Ford got sidetracked in 1973 by a job as a reporter at the *Asbury Park (N.J.) Press.* She has been a writer ever since. After several decades as a journalist and freelance writer and as an editor at four magazines, in 1997 she turned her attention to writing books. A frequent contributor to *Publishers Weekly* and several Web sites, she is also a public speaker, as well as a teacher at churches and writers' conferences around the country. She and her husband, John, live in Central Florida and have two daughters, Elizabeth and Sarah.

Traditions of the Ancients is her seventeenth book.